MW01277327

After
C. T. STUDD

BY

NORMAN P. GRUBB

Author, *C. T. Studd* and
*With C. T. Studd in
Congo Forests*

ZONDERVAN PUBLISHING HOUSE
GRAND RAPIDS, MICHIGAN

COPYRIGHT, MCMXLVI, BY
ZONDERVAN PUBLISHING HOUSE

Printed in the United States of America

EIGHT FORTY-SEVEN OTTAWA AVENUE
GRAND RAPIDS, MICHIGAN

'LET US GO UP AT ONCE AND POSSESS IT'

C. T. Studd launched 'the New Crusade' to unevangelized lands. A year after his death in 1931, in face of mountainous difficulties, the vanguard of a new army began marching out to many fields. A cartoon of the first ten was drawn by Mr. Charlton Smith, which he has superimposed on the last photo of the old warrior

CONTENTS

5

CONTENTS

FOREWORD TO NORTH AMERICAN EDITION

READERS of this account of the results of C. T. Studd's work will praise God for advance in many fields. It is now six years since the book was first written and since then still greater things have been accomplished. The Author says, "God has greatly increased and prospered the work of the Worldwide Evangelization Crusade in its various fields and branches during these years in spite of the fact that they have been war years. Indeed, it has been God's abundant answer to the prayer of faith deliberately made on the day war was declared — the petition that we might be enabled by these dark days to prove and bear testimony to the God who commands the light to shine out of darkness. On this basis, we specifically asked for advance in every phase of the work. Progress has been apparent in personnel, finances, fields and at home, and in the addition of an entirely new branch—the Christian Literature Crusade."

A few paragraphs at the end of each chapter have been added to tell of several of these increases. A more complete account will be published later.

ALFRED W. RUSCOE

Worldwide Evangelization Crusade
8864 Germantown Avenue
Philadelphia 18, Pa.

This book is dedicated to God's hidden servants, who, by prayer and gift and other ways known only to Him, have been co-labourers with Him and us in reaching with the Gospel some of the world's unevangelized millions.

CHAPTER I

THE STORM BREAKS

I WAS sitting on the edge of C. T. Studd's native bed. We were in his bamboo house in the heart of the Ituri Forest. It was 3 a.m. He looked very white and drawn. His thin legs beneath the blankets were drawn up under his chin, with his wasted arms clasped round them. Without was the still African night, the palm trees looking lovely—silhouetted against the moonlit sky—and behind the dark rim of the primeval forest. We had been talking for hours.

Suddenly he said, 'This looks like the end of everything. I don't see any way out.' After a pause he added ' Eighteen years ago God told me to found this mission. We have had all sorts of difficulties, but He has brought me through them all. If God doesn't deliver me now, when I am near the end and faced with the biggest, well, He is . . . But He isn't, because He will ! '

It was the darkest chapter in the mission's history. That hateful thing, internal dissension, had raised its head in our ranks and torn the work in half. We were without representation at home. Rumours had spread from mouth to mouth which shook the confidence of many.

Pauline, who is C. T. Studd's youngest daughter and my wife, had accompanied me on a visit to him

9

in the Congo, knowing that we should not see him again on earth. While we were there, the storm broke. It would be neither helpful nor necessary to go further into the details of the controversy. It has long since been left behind. The love of Christ has swallowed up bitterness and rivalry, nor is it for us to assess the rights and wrongs. God has richly blessed our brethren who formed a new society, even as He has been pleased to bless us.

The point was the severity of the catastrophe. That midnight scene shows even the man of God, C. T. Studd, staggering for a moment under the blow, although rapidly returning to faith. The inward conflict which Pauline and I suffered was intense, as we faced our call to return to England and rebuild in the dense fog of suspicion, condemnation and controversy. It was the darkest valley of our lives also, and we lived there for six months.

Yet we were to learn, as an old saint once wrote, that ' The way to heaven is through hell.' The more the Lord plans to use an instrument, the fiercer the fire in which it is tempered. We had earnestly sought for ten years that we might be instruments meet for His use, and the answer had been a great deal of pruning with very little fruit. Now at last, right from ' the belly of hell,' we were to be lifted up into ' a large place.'

We were praying together four months after our return, when Pauline turned to me on her knees and said, ' Father has gone home. I know it. We are to start anew with God.' I knew it too. We were

dumb with the shock for a time. But it was God's
voice. We left that room different people. We had
heard and accepted God's call. Shortly after, a
cablegram was handed to us at the breakfast table.
We glanced at each other before we opened it, for
we guessed its contents : 'Bwana (C. T. Studd)
glorified July 16th.'

Prepared thus by the Spirit, we knew what lay
before us. We were to take up the sword C. T. Studd
had laid down. Something else had also happened in the blackness of that night. Some of ' the
treasures of darkness,' of which Isaiah speaks, had
been laid open to us, and one supremely great secret
of effective service had become vividly real to us,
which lies at the root of most that follows in these
pages. It was the answer to that simple but fundamental problem, how can I know God's will ? If
I know it, then obviously I can believe and act.
But first I must know.

How can I put the light we saw in a word ?
Perhaps best by describing what we did. We made
one change in the daily programme at headquarters,
but that change made all the difference. It was
customary to start the day's work with a half-hour of
Scripture reading and prayer ; then followed the
real business, letters, interviews, and committees.
Now the emphasis was to be changed. The
reading and prayer was to be the real business of
the day, and the rest fit in as best it might. In
other words, our first occupation became, not to
exercise our own minds, but to find His mind.

What an overwhelming difference that made. Away
went worries, plans, defeatist fears. In their place
was just this. What does God say about it?
What God says is always original, always in the
impossible, and great enough to be worthy of Him.
What He said was this. Our petty human thinking was occupied with the littleness, poverty, weakness of our condition. He said, ' Look at Joshua
and see what I did for him, and Moses and Abraham
and Daniel. Do you think I have given you a great
commission—to evangelize the world—and not
great resources to do it with? Does not all the Bible
tell you that I have come to make people strong out
of their weakness, if they will only believe? Now,
will you believe?'

The answer was obvious. Just one thing remained. For what specifically should we ask and
believe? What was our immediate equivalent of
Moses's need of manna, or Joshua's need of a way
across Jordan? That was not hard to find. Men
and money, of course. For we were a Crusade to
evangelize unoccupied areas, and that needs just
those two supplies.

So we came to our first transaction of faith,
based on guidance, a truly memorable moment in
our history, for what we did then we were to repeat
in an endless succession of instances for an endless
variety of needs. We came somehow to the conclusion, I can't tell exactly how, that for us the impossible which would glorify God and extend His Gospel
would be the supply of ten new workers and all the

12

money for them in a year, by the first anniversary of
C. T. Studd's death, July 16, 1932.

Having done that, we exactly obeyed the word of
Christ, ' When ye pray, believe that ye receive.' We
deliberately thanked the Lord for what we had then
received. From that day on we never asked
again for the ten, but daily reminded Him and ourselves in His presence that they were ours, and
thanked Him. Our daily prayer meetings were
turned into enjoyment meetings, possessing and
enjoying our possessions in the invisible, before we
had them in the visible. One other lesson also that
was gradually learned, of deep importance in faith,
was that the Source is our concern, not the channel :
in other words, that we are to keep occupied with
what we have already received from Him in the
unseen, and not be diverted into looking around for
the way in which He may send it in the seen.

Now for the story of how the ten came. Some
readers may think, ' Well, ten is not many, nor the
£1,500 necessary for their outgoing.'[1] No, they are
not : but remember we were infants learning to
crawl ! To us it had all the thrills of new adventure
and discovery. As we used this one and only method
of obtaining things from God according to His word,
by the invisible hand of faith reaching into His
equally invisible resources, we felt all the joys of
pioneering in a new country.

The first two came in quite easily and soon sailed.
It was then that we saw another condition of the

[1] £1 equals approximately $5.

13

pathway of faith, which is not exactly the faith itself, but is the works which prove the faith to be real and establish us in it. It is the equivalent of the confession with the lips commanded by the Scripture as a necessity for salvation, side by side with the belief in the heart (Rom. x. 9). We saw that one who really believes is ready to make public acknowledgment that the things he has received by faith are his, although he has not yet obtained them in fact. We saw it particularly with Joshua at Jordan. He came out from the presence of God and told his officers to prepare victuals, for in three days they would cross the river. A declaration of a certainty, yet only a certainty to faith. In the same way God told us to write to Jack Harrison, C. T.'s successor on the field, and tell him to expect ten new workers within the year, although owing to the circumstances the missionaries on the field had no thought of immediate increase. I had a brief controversy with the Devil about it, as he told me what a fool I should look predicting what would not come to pass, and that as the new secretary in London I should be doing the best thing possible to shake their confidence. Yet of course it had to be done. The unmistakable word of the Lord had come, and the letter was sent.

The next three, women, were ready to go by March, but there was no money. So we gathered together one morning, faced the fact that nothing hindered them going except finance, and made a definite transaction with the Lord that then and there we

14

received it from Him by faith. The three soon had a fine opportunity of making the open declaration of faith. Two of them were going away for the Easter week-end, so they left their addresses with the third, telling her to wire them if the money were provided during the week-end.

On the Saturday we had two guests. They themselves lived by faith, and so we took it for granted that they had no spare stores of money. As a matter of fact for years they had a sum in the bank which they had dedicated to the Lord, but He had never told them what to do with it ! That night before going to bed, in a word of prayer, someone quite naturally mentioned the three. You can imagine the surprise we had next morning when they came down to tell us about this sum and that in that word of prayer God had spoken to both of them separately that the money was for this purpose ! It turned out to be sufficient for two passages. At this point the faith of the third who had remained with us shone out in really remarkable fashion. We made the news known at dinner time and said that we must send the telegrams. She then said, ' Why not wait half an hour ? God may yet send the money for the third passage ' —in spite of the fact that, being Sunday, no post or visitors would be expected. Just at the time she said this, unknown to us, the treasurer had cause to go over to his office, which was closed, and he there found a letter. When opened, it had within it a cheque for £100 ! The telegrams were sent.

These three sailed in May, followed by two in

June, a total of seven. The eighth arrived from
Canada. Six weeks remained and no applications,
and no money. Five weeks, none. Four weeks, no
application, but a gift of £100. Three weeks, still
none. Two weeks, No. 9 applied.

Now there were but days left. Thirteen days,
twelve, eleven, ten. On the evening of the tenth
No. 10 applied. It was at a conference. He had
spent three days in fasting and prayer to be sure of
God's call, and the next day the Lord set a wonderful
seal on his application. A guest at this conference,
who knew nothing about No. 10's offer, was praying
before breakfast. The Lord distinctly led him to
take a blank cheque from his cheque book and put
it in his pocket, but did not reveal the reason. At
breakfast he heard a mention of the application and
at once knew that the cheque was for this purpose.
Shortly after £120 was in the Secretary's hands.

Two days later two of us were in Ireland. We
went into the matter together and found that £200
was still needed to complete the sum. So we agreed
in secret to ask the Lord for this. A couple of days
after, as we came out of a meeting, our hostess handed
one of us a telegram, and, although she had not an
idea about our secret prayer, said, of all things in the
world, ' Perhaps there is £200 in it.' It was from
London and read, ' Two hundred pounds for the
Ten.'

Within six days of the anniversary God had sent
the ten and all the funds. It never had been our
intention to get this number actually to the field by

[To face p. 16]

EXTRACT FROM A LETTER BY C. T. STUDD

This was written on the journey to the heart of Africa in 1913—the year of the founding of the W.E.C. These few sentences enshrine the principles which lie at the root of all the work of the Crusade. (The slight blur is due to the fact that only a carbon copy of the letter has survived.)

that date, for we felt there must be no hurry about the necessary testing of their suitability. All that we had asked and received from the Lord by faith had been graciously and completely provided. All the ten sailed to the Congo by the autumn, five men and five women. Our joy was great, yet greater and of more importance was the realization that we had been allowed to prove by personal experiment that this was the way outlined by God's word for the fulfilment of His purposes through human agency.

CHAPTER II

C. T. STUDD'S LAST PRAYER

AT the time of their marriage in China, that topsy-turvy couple, Mr. and Mrs. C. T. Studd, had celebrated the day, not by receiving gifts, but by giving one—all they had to God. Before his marriage, on receipt of his inheritance from his father's estate, he had heard God's call to follow literally the command of Christ to the rich young ruler, ' Sell all that thou hast, and give to the poor, and thou shalt have treasure in heaven : and come, take up thy cross and follow Me.' He had obeyed up to the point of distributing all his property (about £30,000) between various Gospel agencies, with the exception of £2,000, which he withheld as a dowry for his bride. When Priscilla Stewart heard of this, she said, ' Charlie, what command did the Lord give you concerning your money ? ' ' To sell all.' ' Have you done so ? ' ' Well, yes, with the exception of this £2,000 that I am giving you.' ' Charlie,' she said, ' I am not going to marry a disobedient man. Either you obey completely or you don't have me.'

So the last £2,000 went as a gift to General Booth, accompanied by a letter from the young couple, in which they said, ' I am instructing our bankers to sell out our last earthly investment and send what they realize to you. Henceforth our bank is in heaven. You see we are rather afraid—

notwithstanding the great earthly safety of Messrs. Coutts and the Bank of England—we are, I say, rather afraid that they may both break on the Judgment Day. Now this does not come from me, for I was told that the Bible says, " He that provideth not for his own house hath denied the faith and is worse than an infidel." So I just took the whole pot and gave it to my little wife wherewith to provide for the household. And so it is now she who sends this money, regarding Heaven as the safest bank, and moreover thinking it is so handy ; you have no trouble about cheques or rates of exchange, but just, " Ask and receive, that your joy may be full." (Signed) My wife and me.'

C. T.'s life story describes the provision of their faithful God for themselves and their four girls through the forty years of their wedded life, at times in poverty, at times in abundance, but always sufficient for daily needs. The point that interests us now is the persistence of faith which C. T. had in the promise that if he had given all to God he could claim ' a hundredfold ' return in this life (Matt. xix. 29). ' You see,' he used to say, ' if I look after the salvation of God's family He will look after the salvation of mine.'

The four girls decided for Christ in their teens. When grown up all married men in the Lord's work, but his eldest daughter became a widow in 1913, and during the war became the bride of a brilliant soldier of King George, but by no means of King Jesus. C. T., whose heart always went out to courage of any kind, and who loved a real man, had great affection for this son-in-law whom he was never to meet on earth. With affection went quenchless faith. Other Christian relatives showed alarm and concern, but he just took it for granted that the Father, to Whom he had given a life's devotion, would never fail him in giving him the final desire of his heart, a family united in Christ. ' David will come in,' he would say, ' and then God will get the use of the ability and courage which only his king and country have had up till now.'

Those of us who knew David at home cannot say that it looked like it ! I am afraid we thought him a hopeless case ; yet there is no man living that can withstand the power of faith. Having risen from sergeant to lieut.-colonel in the Great War, with his name on the list for promotion to brigadier-general when it ended, and gaining as he passed from rank to rank a whole string of decorations, D.C.M., M.C., D.S.O., medal of St. George of Russia 1st class, two mentions in despatches, he finally retired with the rank of lieut.-colonel in the Gordon Highlanders, to take up farming in Rhodesia.

The old problem of parents abroad and a child at home decided them to sell out and they returned to England in 1929. While deciding on their next step they came to live at No. 17, Highland-road, which was their father's home and always open to them, but was also the Crusade head-quarters in London. The lion was trapped, but all so naturally. The one who could not be reached by the unreality of talk was to see for himself the reality of Christian living. Nothing was said to him directly for six months, and then there was only one indecisive conversation. But the walls of Jericho were crumbling, and the last letter which C. T. received on earth in the heart of Africa was to tell him that the last member of his family circle would meet him on the other side, 'made nigh by the blood of Christ.'

' I gradually had my eyes opened to my own personal need of salvation,' said Colonel Munro. ' I am not of a very yielding disposition, but the Lord has His own way of dealing with people, and in spite of myself I began to see that there was more in religion than I had thought. The desire was born in me to really know God, as others said they knew Him. I then asked the Lord to forgive all my transgressions, but I could not honestly say that as result of this I felt any particular change in myself. Thinking that perhaps I had not done it in a right way, I kept on asking for forgiveness and hoping for the best, until one evening, when exercising the dog, I, in desperation, asked the Lord to come and dwell in me and keep me from all sin. At once I knew that my request had been answered, and thereafter the Lord meant something to me that I had never dreamt of before. Now, praise the Lord, I know that He lives ; I know what it feels like to have God in my life ; and I know that even I by His grace and power can be of some use to Him.'

There were no half measures with him. Just as C. T. prophesied, he began to fight in the ranks of God's army as effectively as he had done in the British Army. At that time of our need, he became honorary business secretary of the Crusade, and, with Miss Walder and Miss Muller, our office secretaries, took in hand all that side of the work. He never felt that this was his permanent call, but gave his whole time to it for the next two and a half years, and then moved out to the oversight of evangelistic work among soldiers, while still remaining our treasurer. To-day he is secretary of the Evangelization Society. At this critical moment, by one stroke, the Lord answered C. T.'s final prayer for his family and gave us a much-needed manager of our practical affairs.

CHAPTER III

FROM STRENGTH TO STRENGTH

'HAVE you ever heard 10,000 people shout "Hallelujah"? We have just had the greatest Christmas of our lives' (wrote Mr. von Staden). 'We came here for the annual conference. Fifty missionaries and 10,000 natives gathered. I have never seen a more out and out number of missionaries. They have the fire of the Holy Ghost. During the meetings there is a prayer room all the time. No wonder that miracles are happening. The spirit of sacrifice of their glorified leader is here. When company after company of natives arrived, singing hymns and shouting "Hallelujah," our hearts were deeply touched and we shed tears of joy. Can one ever forget the feeling of standing before 10,000 souls waiting to be fed?'

South African friends, Mr. and Mrs. von Staden, had arrived at Ibambi, in the heart of Africa, in time for the great 'makutano' in 1933. Never had they seen such a sight in their lives. Those forest glades that had echoed through the centuries with the shouts of the drunken revellers, the weird cries of the devil doctors, the ghastly wailing of pagan mourners, were vibrating with the tramp of a new army and ringing with the melody

HEART OF AFRICA
BELGIAN CONGO

23

of a new song, the glory songs of the redeemed, the praises of Him who had called them out of darkness into His marvellous light.

'I shall never forget that day (wrote Edith Moules, one of the missionaries). I am sure that you cannot adequately imagine the sight. The roads were all black with people. First one crowd would arrive, and then another, and as each appeared their hallelujahs rent the air. Forty-five of the lepers from Nala came, having walked, in spite of their crippled limbs, for about 50 miles. My! It was a sight to see them all.'

No building could contain them, but a great open-air church was roughly erected in a square of mango trees, 70 yards by 30. 'Thousands of poles were cut and carried from the forest, also bamboo and leaves without number (wrote Ivor Davies). The poles were made to stand in the ground in long rows, then bamboos tied across the tops of them, and over these thousands of palm branches. The whole had the appearance of a large carpet and proved an excellent shade from the sun.'

'The ground was black with people (wrote Mr. Harrison, who had taken Mr. Studd's place as field leader), yet, in spite of the tremendous numbers, they were not at all out of hand. Dead silence and perfect reverence during prayer, and attentiveness and responsiveness to the messages showed that God was with us in power. It is all so beyond description. The crowds, the beaming faces, the eagerness, the singing, the roars of hallelujahs. One could only

24

stand before them amazed and awed. To see the multitudes dispersing after each meeting was something to be long remembered. Perfect stillness during the benediction, followed by another brief pause and then the thousands stood on their feet.

'Native-like they carried their small stools and chairs above their heads as they left, and so to us on the platform it just looked like a great waving forest of arms. At night time the sleeping places were worth seeing. Inside, every available inch was packed tight with human beings ; outside, hundreds of little fires peeped out of the dark. Those in one shed would be singing some hymn quite different from the people in the next shed, and so it was impossible at a distance to tell what they were singing with so many tunes going at once. The whole station night and day was just vibrating with prayers and praises.'

Near that tremendous scene was a quiet spot, shaded by palm trees. Beneath them was a simple oblong block of concrete. Here had been laid two years before the earthly remains of the man who, seventeen years previously, had been the first messenger of Christ to penetrate these regions and had written home, ' Day after day they run along in front and behind our cycles, shouting, laughing and singing their chants ; you never heard such a din nor saw so great enthusiasm. It was like an excited crowd surging round the pavilion at the conclusion of a great cricket match. They didn't speak Bangala and we didn't speak Swahili, so we had to talk dumb-crambo. Fancy, there were hundreds of them all round us, sometimes 500, all running ; we often cycled fast too, but the women and girls ran and laughed and shouted as fast and loudly as the men and boys. Well, here is our " Eldorado." Here is a land and a people to whom the Blessed Name has never been known throughout all time. Shall we leave them thus ? We will not. We will sell our pottage and buy therewith our birthright to declare the glory of God to this people. They shall hear and hear to purpose by the power of the Holy Ghost.'

C. T. Studd was not beneath that block of concrete. With ' the great cloud of witnesses ' we have no doubt that he was sharing full-throated in the worship and praise of that African concourse, and with what inconceivable triumph and adoration as he looked on the fruits of obedience, toil and daring faith, and worshipped the Saviour who gave the grace for it. In his own lifetime he had seen crowds of 4,000, but here were 7,000, and then 10,000. Life out of death indeed !

Go back a few years and contrast the early lives of some of those rejoicing thousands, and the kind of conditions that C. T. Studd met with when he first entered the Ituri forest. They are almost incredible. Is it any wonder that these dark-skinned folks need long patience, and that with some the light is very dim, and with some the feet very stumbling ? Barnepetia was at the conference —with no ears. ' One day the Medjes came to my village to kill and eat (he told Mary Rees, whom

26

he accompanied on her evangelistic treks). My mother put me on her back and ran with me for life. An enemy followed and stuck her in the back with a spear. Afterwards they cut up my mother into pieces. I saw them with my own eyes, and I saw my mother's blood all around. Said one man, "Take the child away from his mother's blood," and he did ; he wiped my eyes and nose for me, he arranged me very nicely, then he said, "Take the meat, I will take the boy. He shall grow up with me and be my slave." ' One morning at dawn the poor lad thought he would run away. But he was captured, thrashed and put in the stocks. Then, horror of horrors, his owner one day was worse for drink and in a drunken frenzy said, ' Because you ran away, I will cut off your ears.' ' So he took me from the stocks and cut off my ears and my body was covered with blood.' Years after, the earless lad heard of Jesus through Miss Roupell, the senior missionary of the Crusade, his sorrow was turned into joy, and his radiant testimony is, ' I desire that all the people in the world shall know Jesus Christ. I rejoice because of the blood of Jesus Christ. I rejoice in Jesus only. God is my God because He saved me. I want all to be saved like me.'

Fulani was doubtless at the conference also. She has no hands. Sold as a child to be the wife of ' a disagreeable old head man, ill-kempt, dirty, and not often sober, she was a slave of the older wives (writes Edith Moules), but most of all she hated from the bottom of her heart her horrible old husband.

27

She ran away. Caught and brought back, she ran away again. This time her husband was really angry. He tied her wrists together very tightly with strong native rope, then he suspended the shrieking child by the ends of that rope to the rafters of an old hut. But this was not all. He beat the little wriggling form with a whip and left her hanging there suspended by the wrists for two whole nights.

'She was taken down at last, and the burst, bleeding and suppurating arms were bound up native fashion, but later one hand sloughed right off to the wrist and the other was shrunken and twisted permanently out of shape. This all happened some years ago and the old husband is now dead. Fulani is happily married and has a dear wee babe of her own. How she manages him with no hand one is left to wonder, but her cheerfulness is amazing and would put many to shame. It has often been said, " Why bother about the heathen ? " but as Fulani goes about, gripping her dear babe with those awful wrists, this poor little woman still speaks to me of benighted souls without the Gospel and the command, " Go ye . . . and preach the Gospel to every creature "—and that includes such as the old husband.'

Turn again from these ghastly scenes and come on a visit to another village. It is a quiet scene this time, for a happy sense of peace and order pervades the place. The open spaces between the huts are nicely swept. The men and women have lost that dull and sullen look common to this part of Africa.

28

Over there that thatched building is a church.
Children can be heard repeating verses of Scripture. Over here from this shed comes the busy clang
of hammer on anvil. We might expect any moment
to see a missionary cross this quiet compound. But
no ; no white man has ever lived here, but the Prince
of Peace Himself has made the hearts of many of its
inmates His dwelling place, and there lies the secret.
This is the village of Mamayangu ('My mother')—
now in glory with C. T. Studd—the native blacksmith whose reputation with Government officials
was that they had never seen another like him and
whose light shone out to distant chiefdoms. Well
has he been called ' one of Congo's greatest Christians.' Yet there was nothing outstanding in him as
a man. He was much like hundreds of others, with
this one difference, God had all the way in his life.

One day two missionaries passed his forge on a
journey, and looked in—a memorable day. ' We
could not but notice (they wrote) the interest paid
to us by Mamayangu.' Nor can we guess at the
amazement and dawning light on that dark soul as
he drank in for the first time the story of God's love.
One of the two men, impressed by Mamayangu's
response, re-visited him. ' I asked him whether he
received what we had said. To my surprise he said,
" I received the Good Words when you were here
before." ' The God who loves to save in a moment
of time had entered this man's heart after one hearing of the Gospel. Most notable of all, the fact
that makes him so outstanding as a Christian, these

two short interviews were practically all that missionaries had to do with his spiritual growth. Through the Spirit and the Word alone he developed into the missionary bishop of that area.

Above all else he was a man of the Book, but first he had to teach himself to read. He did this in original fashion. He obtained a New Testament from a native in a trader's shop, but of course had not the faintest idea of the meaning of those queer looking objects on the pages. So he waited daily in his village until he saw some natives pass, whom he could recognize as in Government or traders' employment. Then he called out, ' Here, stop a minute. You look hot and hungry. Come and have some food.' When the victim was well settled before a good meal out came the precious book. ' By the way, you can read, can't you ? Can you just tell me how to pronounce this, and this, and this ? ' Then that piece of information was conned over until the next likely native passed that way. This continued until he could read.

Separation from the world soon followed, from polygamy through two of his wives leaving him because of his testimony, and from drink and dancing as he read that ' men love darkness rather than light because their deeds are evil.' ' Well,' he said, ' if we always drink and dance in the darkness, it must be evil, therefore, if I am going to be a true follower of the Lord Jesus Christ, I must forsake these things.' God took the desire for them completely away, and he became the first man of his tribe to uplift the standards of Christian family life amid all the vileness around.

Far more than that, capacities once enslaved by sin and self-indulgence were now at the disposal of the Spirit for a unique work, and he became the founder and head not merely of an indigenous church, but of the equivalent to a missionary society, sending out and supporting its own workers to distant places. The very village was remodelled and became so like a mission station in its character and activities that when Mr. Harrison was once visiting there and was speaking to a passing official, the latter spoke of Mamayangu as ' a paid worker of the mission, and as if the church and other buildings had been put up by us. He was amazed when I said that all he saw there was the voluntary efforts of Mamayangu and his Christians. At first he did not grasp it all. He said, " But this is your station." I said it was not and that we had no place there.'

God took Mamayangu quite suddenly. ' He was white through and through, one of God's gentlemen (wrote Mr. Jack Scholes, the assistant field-leader, who had been like a brother to him). We never had any qualms or doubts about Mamayangu's salvation. He was always the same, red-hot for Jesus. We have lost a dearly beloved brother, but we know we shall meet again.'

Spurred on by his example, and by the gradually growing conviction of years, our workers saw a new era in our Congo field in 1937—the establishment of the native church on completely indigenous lines. Mr. Harrison found all his missionary workers at one with him.

'This is the thing which we have been praying for and looking forward to for years (wrote Jack Scholes), and now praise God it is coming into being. Once given the opportunity the native Christians will, we are sure, rise to their responsibility and prove to be real pillars in the church. The time has come when they must increase and we missionaries decrease.'

The ensuing years have given abundant proof of the rightness of this decision. Each of the older stations has rejoiced to see the natives taking full control of all church affairs. 'There was a local conference with about 1,000 natives (wrote Muriel Harman) concerning the Ibambi group of churches. The most thrilling thing was the native church in action—the meeting of the elders. The church was crowded with all those who wanted to listen. We didn't get breakfast until mid-day, but it was worth it ! The wisdom they showed was remarkable, and they quoted Scripture for almost everything, and made judgments which, while they were surprising, one felt were right.'

'The greatest blessing I got was in listening to the native elders discussing church affairs (writes Ellen Shaw). Not one said, "I think this or that," but, " the Word of God teaches thus and thus." My heart was filled with joy as I listened to them.'

Side by side with this new era in the older areas

has been a determined march forward to complete the occupation of the regions beyond, until at each point of the compass we have reached the boundaries of neighbouring missions. From a round 10,000 square miles occupied during C. T. Studd's life-time, the work has now spread over 60,000, although the increase of missionary staff from thirty-five to fifty-five makes it plain that the new occupation is still incomplete, and fresh workers are needed.

Each advance is an epic of its own, but it will need a separate book to describe them. There was the daring venture of lame Zamu, who limped 200 miles with his wife to a strange tribe, and was followed by Jim and Mrs. Grainger, who opened the centre at Opienge. There was the 100-mile stride beyond Opienge again, through the gorilla forest to Lubutu, where tribes, still only partly subdued, are being reached by Harold Coleman and Colin Buckley.

There are Fred and Mrs. Dunbar, who have spent the first year of their married life without seeing another white person, among perhaps the lowest forest tribe we have touched, a semi-pigmy people called the Walesi ; they have shown an extreme indifference, but here and there already give signs of coming triumphs. There was the advance to Kesanga, an area on which we had our eyes for ten years, until one day, when studying the map together, Mr. Harrison asked Mr. Scholes, 'You see this place that Bwana (C. T. Studd) so often pointed out to us? Will you put your finger on it and I will also put mine ? For if we ask in the name of Jesus, we can have for God's glory those things that are needful for His work.' Within a year a visit had been paid by Harold Williams, the work opened by Percy Moules, and to-day Vernon and Mrs. Willson, after some years of hard going, are seeing the first fruits.

Then there is Harry Jones, who rose from what most thought would be his death-bed, renewed in vigour and vision, to penetrate the blackest of black forest to Kondolole, where the undergrowth was so thick that in measuring the site for the station they could not push their way in to discover what there was by way of a water supply ; and to think that within four years the station was cleared, houses and church built, and that 120 natives had courage and zeal enough to come the month's journey on foot to the great conference at Ibambi. Having an evil reputation as robbers and raiders in their old life, who would believe in the change and let them pass in peace ? Still come they did, fascinated like children to see so many white people and so many marvels such as the motor car, and impressed beyond all to be among a vast concourse of natives from various tribes mingling in brotherly love. What could be a more amazing proof to such as these of the power of God ?

Finally, there is the newest advance of Robert and Mrs. Milliken to the keen, intelligent Babuas, among whom they have used a new method of evangelism with eminent success, by remaining for a period

34

in each central village and giving consecutive teaching. Out of a year of married life they have spent ten months as 'Gospel tramps.'

Then there are those whose lives are each an epic in themselves. Single women called out from behind a counter or from a farm or quiet home, who have now spent years preaching, teaching, healing, building, planting, going lonely Gospel treks, far in excess of the activities and responsibilities of an ordained minister at home: Esmé Roupell, our senior worker, who was in charge of a station with a congregation of 500, sending out fifty of its own evangelists: Lilian Dennis, handling native conferences of 2,000 at Deti, a beloved mother to hundreds in the villages around: Mary Rees, ever on the tramp for those seeking the light, penetrating witchcraft dens, winning cannibals for Christ's kingdom: Ellen Shaw, small in stature but full of the Holy Ghost, in charge of Nala with twenty groups of believers in nearby villages: Daisy Kingdon, Canada's No. 1, a tower of strength and wise counsel, spending much of her time in the villages round Wamba: Muriel Harman, the servant of all for Jesus' sake, who, besides her labours with the natives, is called here and there for weeks at a time when missionaries need medical attention: Agnes Chansler from the United States, devoted to Africa's children.

All these single women, who lived and worked with C. T. Studd, are living evidences of the truth that in Christ ' there is neither male nor female,' and that by the enduement of the Holy Ghost women receive the courage of men, as men receive the gentleness of women.

Others, not already mentioned, who were among those gathered round C. T. Studd's grave in 1931, and who had gained by contact with him a quality of abandonment distinctive even among our own ranks, are Jack Scholes, assistant leader to Jack Harrison, who with his wife has in the last seven years built up Poko, now one of the strongest centres of the indigenous church : Herbert and Mrs. English who have refused to give in at our most difficult station, Niangara, the strongest centre of Romanism and materialism ; Harold and Mrs. Williams from Australia, beloved of all for laying aside their desire to work among the people during their first eight years, in order to manage the motor transport of the mission and make the work of others more easy, now in charge of Wamba ; Percy and Mrs. Moules giving their lives to the lepers [1] ; Jack and Lily Roberts, brother and sister, God's instruments in an outpouring of the Spirit at Imbai [2] ; Sam Elder, and Herman Meyer of U.S.A., pioneers in the Kesanga district, spending months on the move among the villages.

What more can we say than to praise and worship Him, who by His Spirit and example makes apostles out of very ordinary folk ? The Congo is our mother field. In a peculiar way it has the marks of our

[1] See 'My Neighbour' by Edith Moules, price 3d. (10c.)
[2] See 'Floods on Dry Ground' by Eva Stuart Watt, price 1s. (35c.)

36

beloved founder on it, and thank God that the motto by which he was inspired is still the battle cry of his successors, ' If Jesus Christ be God and died for me, then no sacrifice can be too great for me to make for Him.'

CHAPTER IV

CLIMBING

THE ladder of faith is only climbed rung by rung. Back in London, God now spoke to Pauline and me on a personal matter. It would be no concern of this book were it not that it had far-reaching consequences. According to normal custom, we had always received our monthly share of what the Lord sent in to the Crusade, and which is equally divided among all ; but the Lord spoke to us concerning this question. Neither Mr. nor Mrs. Studd had ever received money from the mission for personal needs, and now that we were called to take their place at the home base ought we not to follow their example ?

Another point also carried weight with us. We wanted to share further with our fellow-Crusaders on the fields in their life of sacrifice. There were plenty of risks and hardships out there, but all so ' cushy ' at home. This seemed a means of doing it on a very small scale, besides preserving more of the mission gifts for their real purpose—the fields abroad. We took the step and, needless to say, have since proved the daily faithfulness of God.

The real importance of this action was only seen later. Very soon we felt the need of a co-worker. We wanted to challenge God's people with the vision and commission of world-wide evangelization, but I was too occupied at headquarters. If the Lord would send a deputation worker, that would solve the problem. Here lay the difficulty. How could we divert funds for such a worker when we had just resigned our own allowances to avoid using the mission money? Again the solution was obvious —that God should provide a deputation worker on the same faith basis.

Now we began to see why the Lord had thus led us. If the Lord would do this, then here would be the nucleus of a headquarters staff on new lines, none of whom would be a charge on mission funds. On that basis we need not restrict the number of home workers, but have all we want, and form a faith fellowship at home which could bear its own testimony and carry its own message to the homeland, side by side with the workers on the field.

Once more we plunged in. This time our request was well hedged round with necessary conditions. We wanted a deputation worker, but he must have qualifications. He should have been in the Congo and able to speak from first-hand knowledge of the work; he should be unfit to return; and he should not require an allowance! I shall give the answer in detail, not because it is more wonderful than many others, but because it was the first of its kind, and set the ball rolling for the formation of faith staffs on all home bases, who already number twenty-eight.

I had arranged visits to a few cities to hold thanksgiving meetings for the life of C. T. Studd. One of them was at Liverpool. There was a good audience of 1,000, but one face near the front particularly attracted my attention. It was Alfred Ruscoe, whom I had known and loved in the Congo in years gone by, but who had left the mission and become a critic of C. T. Studd and the work. Now a piece of good news had reached me, that he had recently had a wonderful experience of the filling of the Holy Ghost after years of darkness, and that the Lord had shown him that his wilderness experience had been due to his leaving the Crusade. The friend who told me added that he believed that he was the one I needed as a co-worker. I turned the suggestion down as unthinkable, for I felt sure it would be misunderstood on the field.

Yet how perfectly God works out His plans. My reaction to Ruscoe sitting there in front of me at the meeting was one of annoyance. I felt he would be sure to criticize what I should say, and consequently I did not have much liberty that night! 'But at least,' I thought, 'I shan't see " Rusiko " afterwards. He will hardly stop and speak.' Yet, lo and behold, at the close of the meeting he was among the first on the platform ! I took his hand and sat down to talk. I got up to speak to someone, and as I did so I said, 'What are you doing now?' 'Nothing in particular,' he replied. 'Well, you had better come and help me,' I said, and could have bitten my tongue off a moment later. I had said the very thing I had told my friend I could never say ! Yet somehow I knew it was of God.

I could see Ruscoe was just as much put out as I was, although little did I know the reason. For, eighteen months before, God had told him through a verse of Scripture that he had a special work for him. Time passed, nothing turned up, and, yielding to the pressure of friends, he had just decided to be ordained, when my invitation came to him ' out of the blue ' and he knew it to be God's call.

The Holy Ghost had beautifully prepared us both and then drawn us—into a fellowship which, as this book will show later, was to have such far-reaching consequences.

Yet even then I fondly thought there were plenty of loopholes for escape. He would not seriously want to come back; besides, what about an allowance? We talked again and in spite of ourselves we both felt drawn still more to it. We arranged to meet at Derby, near his home, where I had a meeting. It was a small gathering, without much blessing, I thought. Afterwards we went to the station to catch our respective trains. We arrived to find that both had gone. We went back to the ticket office to make further inquiries for night trains, when a stranger broke in and said, ' If you two gentlemen want to stay the night, there are very cheap rooms to be obtained in that café yonder.' That settled it. Thrown together again !

We talked on into the early hours of the morning. Ruscoe fulfilled two of the conditions; he had been on the field and was unfit to return, having had three attacks of blackwater fever ; but I said to myself, ' There's one thing certain, he will never agree to our position of faith, so I am still safe.' Nor did I mention the subject to him. Then down went my last defence. He suddenly introduced the subject of faith and said, ' There's one condition which I should have to lay down if I came in. I have been working with George Fox's Evangelistic Band, and have had such blessing in the life of faith that I could not go back to receiving an allowance.' That finished me !

The next morning, while we were having break-fast in the café, Ruscoe made one further remark. He said, ' There is one seal left which I asked of God ; it was that He would give definite blessing in the meeting last night.' A few minutes later the door bell rang, and a woman entered with a parcel under her arm. She was the woman who had arranged the meeting, and I don't know to this day how she discovered where we had been staying. She came to say that I had left a parcel of literature behind. She also said that she had a special message for me. A young woman had spoken to her after the meeting and asked her particularly to let me know that, although the meeting was small, it had not been in vain, for she herself would never be the same again ! Ruscoe's last doubt had gone to the winds, and the Lord's answer had been so abundant that we could with confidence ask for all the other workers needed.

CHAPTER V

TO BELIEVE IS TO HAVE

WHEN first we were led to pray for the ten, we already had in mind, as a more distant goal, a memorial in flesh and blood to C. T. Studd—twenty-five new workers. In our weakened situation, and realizing that twenty-five represented an increase of almost three-quarters in our numbers, we had regarded it merely as an aspiration for the future ; but after the vision and realization of the ten, to ask for the remaining fifteen as our next annual objective—by July 16, 1933, the second anniversary—became obvious.

We went about it by the same methods, although we were growing in the use of them. We kept continually before ourselves the fact that, by the eye of faith, we already had the fifteen, and we busied ourselves in daily thanksgiving. How hardly we learn that the invisible is verily the real. If hard facts appear to deny it, down crashes that flimsy, foolish palisade of faith, which calls things that are not as though they were !

Four months of this second year had passed. We had reached the beginning of December, and had naturally thought that by now we should have a flow of candidates and some money, but not one was ready to go out, nor had any money come in. According to the principle before revealed to us, we

had made the simple statement in our magazine
that God would be sending this number by that
given date. The storm troops of unbelief, armed
as always by so-called hard facts, those ' appearances '
by which Jesus told us not to judge, those waves
which were more real to Peter than the Master's
assuring ' Come,' penetrated our defences and wiped
out both spoken word and written declaration. We
had no business to waver. We had yet to learn that
we have only one enemy to fight in this warfare of
faith : not things, not people outside us, but only the
attempts of fear and doubt, those emissaries of Satan,
to get a lodgment within. Our failure on this occasion was a lesson to us, and certainly God's mercy
came half-way to meet us, just as Jesus upheld the
sinking Peter.

I was preparing the January issue of the magazine
and said to the Lord that I could not again publish
the statement that fifteen would be with us by July
unless I had a seal from Him. The final proof had
to go to the printer the next day, so I said, ' If You
will only send me £100 before 11 a.m. to-morrow, I
will take that as the seal. But if You do not, I will
not put in the article.' 11 a.m. came. I had the
proof on the desk in front of me, but no £100. So I
said to the Lord that I was very sorry, but in
these circumstances I must drop the fifteen and
publish nothing further about it. As I said that, I
saw Colonel Munro coming across from the office.
He entered the room waving something in his hand.
It was a cheque from Scotland for £100. The

article went in. The fallacy and weakness of my action, and the mercy of God, are obvious. If the exercise of faith means that first we find the will of God, then we receive our request when we pray (Mark xi. 24), how can we be foolish enough to go about asking for seals on a thing which we have said that we already have ?

Things then began to move. The first three came for the 'Heart of Africa.' Some money arrived in February. By March £250 was still needed, but we were led to publish in the March magazine that they would sail by the next boat without mentioning the financial situation, which meant that the money must be in by March 13. On March 5 came a gift of £100, and on March 11, two days before the time limit, came £150 from the other side of the world.

This was followed by a pregnant revelation. The ten had been only for the 'Heart of Africa,' and we had taken it for granted that the fifteen would be the same. The remark of a friend opened our eyes to the fact that, as God's commission to Mr. Studd was world-wide, the perfect memorial to him would be a world-wide twenty-five. We had already received several applications for other unoccupied fields, but until this moment had not regarded them as within the scope of the memorial twenty-five. Now we saw the full sweep of God's plan, that the first ten should go to the land of Mr. Studd's special labours, and the last fifteen be scattered through many lands and begin to carry out his world-wide vision of occupying every unoccupied

region.   Two came forward for Colombia, two for
Arabia, two for Spanish Guinea, one more for the
Congo, three for Lesser Tibet—a total of thirteen.

The weeks passed.   The Lord sent money for some
of these.   The gift for Pat Symes, our first representative to Colombia, was especially remarkable.
He was to open a new field in this part of South
America.   He had left his home in Australia for
a different destination, so that none who might
normally have helped knew of his need of funds.
We suggested a few meetings in England, but he
received definite guidance from the Lord that he
was not to take meetings with a view to obtaining
financial help, and was to remain at Headquarters
and prove that God was calling him to this new
work by receiving a first £100 direct from Him.
He had a struggle to come and tell me.   He felt that
he ought to say so at the next morning meeting, but
feared and kept silence.   Rebuked in spirit for not
speaking, he came back after the meeting to find me
talking to a woman in the drawing-room.   I introduced him to her, and during a short conversation
he stated what God had told him, and went out.

I had asked him to go and collect some further
information on Colombia from a friend living ten
miles away on the other side of London.   He never
told me that he only had sixpence in the world, but
went on his errand.   Fourpence was spent on getting
there, partly by bus and partly on foot.   On the
return journey he walked to the Thames Embank-
ment, intending to get a twopenny tram ride from

there. A 'down and out' accosted him and asked the price of a cup of coffee. Pat refused, saying that he had only twopence in the world, and passed on. The Spirit told him to go back and speak to the man about his soul. Pat went back, but found that he could not speak about his soul and do nothing for his body, so the twopence changed hands and Pat walked the eight miles home.

Meanwhile I continued my interview with the woman, who was a visitor from the Midlands. She told me that she had £100 which she wanted to go towards the opening of a new field. 'Why,' I said, 'that man who has just spoken to us is the first pioneer to a new field and has asked the Lord for this exact sum.'

Pat arrived back weary and perspiring. I opened the door to him with the cheque of £100 in my hand just at the same time that the Devil had been hard at work telling him that the life of faith was a poor business !

Only six weeks now remained. There were still two more vacancies in the fifteen, and about £500 needed to send them.

On June 15 we went to our annual Worldwide Evangelization Crusade conference. On arrival at the station we were met with the news that two more fully-trained young men had received the call for Colombia. The next day, at a preparatory meeting for the conference, the verse was brought to us, 'If ye abide in Me, and My words abide in you, ye shall ask what ye will, and it shall be done unto you.' The point was pressed home that the person who is consciously abiding is given the privilege of claiming this promise. It was suggested that the audience claim what they specially needed in the way of spiritual blessing in the coming few days. The blessing I needed was £500! I went alone with God, examined whether I was abiding in Him so far as I knew, and received the £500 by faith.

The Lord always tests faith and the test came the following day. For some years I had attended annually some days of prayer in Ireland early in July; but this year I had the conviction that I was not to go away from our watch tower of faith in London before July 16 unless the fifteen were complete. Therefore the only way I could attend would be if the £500 came in at the conference or just after. My hostess in Ireland was at the conference and asked me if I was coming. What was I to say? I said I hoped so. The Lord said, ' That is not faith. Hoping is not believing.' On a later inquiry I tried again and said, ' I will, if the Lord has sent a certain deliverance.' The Lord said, ' There are no "if's" about faith. The Scripture says faith is substance (Heb. xi. 1), and the man of faith acts on faith just as if he had the current coin in his pocket.' Finally, when she asked a third time, the Lord helped me through and I said, ' Yes, I will attend the prayer days, because the deliverance is coming at the conference.'

The last day of the conference came, and not a penny. Next morning we were all dispersing to return home. Farewells were said and people began to leave for the London train. It was found that there were more for this train than was calculated and not enough conveyances. At the last moment several were waiting to go. A large taxi was called. We went in with the party and were driven off at top speed. Half-way along the three-mile journey a tyre went with a bang. We all jumped into a tram, but it was too late. We arrived at the station to find the train had just gone. Ten minutes were taken making fresh arrangements, and then one of those who had lost the train took me aside and said words to this effect, 'It is remarkable that I missed this train, for the Lord told me yesterday that if there was money still needed for the fifteen I was to give £400. I intended to say nothing and catch the train, but now I have lost it and must speak.' We were like they who dream. We felt we must tell someone of this wonderful last minute deliverance, forgetting in the excitement of the moment that it was only a gift of £400, whereas £500 had been asked of God. A Christian friend was manager of a shop near the station, so we went over and out of the fullness of our heart told him the story. We had no sooner finished than he said, 'While you have been speaking, the Lord has told me to give £100.' The £500 was complete.

The fifteen finally consisted of ten men and five women. We much wanted the last of the memorial twenty-five to be a home staff member, and Miss Hand coming in at that time filled the place.

CHAPTER VI

IT COSTS

THE beauties of Colombia, which ravish the eye of the traveller in endless succession, leave him breathless and entranced. This country, least known of the South American Republics, is a tangled mass of mountains; not the naked giants of the North American Rockies, but the green-clothed heights and depths of the tropical Andes. The eye drinks in the freshness of the emerald slopes running down to the torrents thousands of feet below, sees hamlets and villages, set like jewels on the mountain sides, with their groves of 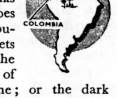 oranges, bananas and sugar cane; or the dark richness of the tropical forests sweeping unbroken up to the skyline, a maze of evergreens, with here and there splashes of bright red or startling yellow when a whole tree is in bloom.

What a difference when the traveller has the eye of the missionary rather than the tourist! While not unmoved by the glories of nature, his interest is centred on the crowning wonder of God's creation, man made in God's image, redeemed by Christ's blood. As he visits city, village and farmstead, he finds dirt, disease, ignorance, fanaticism rampant. By nature the people are kindly and friendly, half

Indian, half Spaniard, with the eager capacity for God common to the Latin races ; but Rome has reached here first. In place of liberty, purity and love for God and man the evil fruits of superstition, priest-control, laxity of morals and of respect for human life have blossomed. Illegitimacy is the sad heritage of one child in every three. Illiteracy abounds, with the consequent intolerance of fresh ideas, accompanied by depressed standards of living.

Faithful missionary work has been carried on for over eighty years, directly reaching some two million of the country's eight million inhabitants, but indirectly many more by the dissemination of Scriptures and tracts. Doubtless this has helped in the thorough, though quiet, political and social revolution now taking place. Now a wise and liberty-loving Government is in power. Smart new administrative buildings are rising, the old-time dusty market squares are giving place to the advent of concrete. An amazing series of roadways have been cut through the mountains. Education is on the increase. Many are casting off their old religious shackles and absorbing modern ideologies, but, alas, loss of faith in priest and church is often accompanied by loss of faith in God.

At such a time as this, but without our knowing of the social revolution quietly taking place, God's call came to us to open work in Colombia, being the most neglected of the South American Republics. Pat Symes, a member of the fifteen and the first

51   D 2

representative of the Crusade, sailed in July, 1933. He crossed three ranges of the Andes to reach the capital, Bogota, one of the highest cities in the world, on an 8,000-feet plateau. Two senior workers of the American Presbyterians, the Rev. and Mrs. A. Allan, were instrumental in obtaining permission from the Government for his entry, and gave him a warm welcome to their home. There, at a missionary conference, Pat made known for the first time the programme which had been revealed to him on board ship, and which he had made his own by an act of faith, that God would send fifty workers in ten years. Such a bold statement by a first worker to a new land took even us by surprise, and we wondered whether the statement was based more on human hopes than divine assurance !

After a period of language study, he and his first co-workers, Nesta Keri Evans, John Harbeson and Harold Wood, all members of the fifteen, made their first centre at Zipaquira, in a region where there were only two points of witness among two and a half millions of people. As soon as they began to preach in the open air they felt the scorching breath of blind fanaticism, ' the time cometh that whosoever killeth you will think that he doeth God service.'

Sometimes the people rushed on the Crusaders like a swarm of angry bees, cursing, stoning, mud-slinging. At Cajica Pat wrote, ' They came down upon us like madmen. They covered us with all the filth that they could find, then began to buffet and push us. We tried to make our way out and they went mad in their fury, punched, pushed and hit. Señora Matilde and I got hit with fists all over the body. I tried to protect Matilde, and when they nearly put me on the ground she lifted me up and got the blows. Nesta got a big stone in the head and bled freely. The police came to our aid and held back the angry crowd. If they had not come you might not have got this letter to-day, for the rage of Satan was in their faces. We do praise God that He has chosen us to suffer a little for Him. We all can say that while we were being beaten we never felt one little bit of hatred in our hearts, nor did we want to hit back. Nesta lost some blood and was very weak from the pain. While I washed her with my handkerchief and water from a pipe, Matilde preached again to the people. She wept, telling them that we had only come out of love and loved them still. We came home and had a praise meeting in the evening. Two weeks later we three men went back again. . . .'

A few years ago public street preaching was not much used because of the fanaticism of the people and certain Government restrictions ; but under the present liberal Government the Crusaders have visited hardly a town or village where they have not met with encouragement and protection from the official classes. The police have attended the meetings, but, although pressed by the authorities, the Crusaders have refused to take action against disturbers. Such an unheard-of attitude has always given great opportunity to witness to the true faith.

The first outstanding trophy of grace was a woman, an ex-actress, the Señora Matilde already referred to, whose husband is paymaster of the gaol at the capital. Her brother-in-law is secretary to the Premier. There were no half measures about her transformation. ' I have been a great sinner,' she publicly testified with tears. ' I was miserable and disgusted with my life and wanted the real religion. In my misery I cried, "God, where art Thou?" Then I met Don Pat (Symes), and he spoke to me of the Holy Spirit and of cleansing through the blood. He opened heaven to me and I knew the Lord Jesus Christ, who took the vessel which was marred and made it again.' The husband remained a cynical scoffer, but a bold step was taken.

She had a passion to work for God and the missionaries accepted her as their first national co-worker, in spite of her husband. In doing so a covenant of faith was made with God that He would save the husband, and they wrote home to tell us that this would surely come to pass, having before-hand testified to the man himself, who laughed the idea to scorn. Three years later God stripped him of his veneer of self-righteousness by bringing to light a life of secret sin. He stormed and raved and declared he would leave his wife, but he returned in a few days a broken man. God had done the work, and he knelt with his wife to confess all and plead for God's mercy. This thorough man of the world, cultured, handsome, able, later broke into tears as he told the missionaries the story of God's grace to him, and he is now, side by side with his wife, witnessing in his office to his own compatriots.

Conversions of this kind began to multiply as the Crusaders mastered the language and scattered to new districts. The next stage was reached in a group of believers coming out for Christ in the town of Viota, country folk who came in weekly with their produce to the market. Ken Green, who had gone to this field in 1934, formed these believers into a little church. Several could read and were given the Scriptures. They elected their own elders and rented a house for a meeting-place, outside which a notice is fixed saying that they are 'the Evangelical Church of Christ.' Ken Green passed on to open work in a new centre, while this little assembly has continued to function as an independent branch of Christ's church according to the standards of the New Testament. Their church funds corresponded to their means of livelihood. 'We now have eight young hens in the care of the believers, who will feed them, selling the eggs and handing in the cash for the church box. We hope to buy a young pig to rear in the same way. Don Filipe (the senior elder) has also given the use of a piece of land up on the mountain to sow vegetables.' The church now numbers fifteen baptized members, who witness faithfully by life, word and tract distribution.

The next development, of great importance for the future, was the founding in 1937 of our first Bible Institute by Ken Green. 'I can't say in words

all the joy that flooded my heart on the first Monday
to see the four fellows at their desks, beginning to
study the Word. To think that a year ago two were
unsaved, and one backslidden and living in adultery. We all live together as Colombians and eat at
the same table, and they are just as real pals as any
English fellows could be. The beds, desks, black-
board were made by two of the students, and the wife
of one of them cooks for us. Morning prayers have
been times of blessing, and the early " repetition "
prayers are disappearing and intense heart-prayers
taking their place.' The Institute received furniture
for a comfortable sitting-room from one of the
wealthiest students, Don Miguel, who, with his
wife and children, was turned out of his home in a
fanatical village. Three students complete their
course at the end of 1939 and go out to work in connection with our missionaries. The number in the
school is about to increase, and the objective of the
Crusaders is to train fifty national workers who, with
the fifty of our own number and in fellowship with
the other missions, can complete the evangelization
of this country.

The range of witness soon widened as the number
of Crusaders increased. In turn were occupied the
towns of Zipaquira, Chiquinquira, Tunja, Choconta, Bogota, Fusagasuga, all these in the mountain
districts ; also Villavicencio, Honda and Giradot
down in the hot country ; and later the more distant
centres of Rio Negro and Socorro. A district like
Chiquinquira, with its surrounding towns, has

about 100,000 souls, and each of the others has
almost as many. Some were opened at risk of
life. Nesta Evans (now Mrs. Wood) wrote from
Choconta : ' I had no peace from morning to night,
boys from the house of the priest threw great big
stones at the door, walls and windows, forcing an
entrance ; but I managed to keep the shutters to
with all my force, or they would have destroyed all
my tracts. The door was smothered with dung at
nights. Finally the poor owner, evidently frightened
by the priest, kindly asked us to go. She feared they
would pull the house to pieces, as the annual feast
days drew near, when all are drunk and fight.

' Being homeless, God moved a heart, a Rahab, to
hide me during the feast days ; but a fanatic saw me
enter the room and began to screech and shout until
the whole street were out to hear. At last they got
to such a fever pitch that the policeman had to take
me out. The mayor sent for me and said I was in
great danger. He refused me a prison cell in which
to hide during the feast days, but at the same time
refused to listen to those who demanded that he
should expel me. So, leaving the mayor, I turned
to God—again homeless. I wended my way to the
shop where I buy my food, and the owner (Señora
Sara) said how sorry she was for all that had happened and asked me to go into her one room behind
the shop. There I remained a week. God knew I
sought His glory and could not leave Choconta, so
He made the impossible possible, touching a heart
which would suffer much if found out. There in that

wee room I hid, in Heaven amid Inferno. At the
other side of the canvas partition, which divided the
bed from the rest of the room, were drunkards and
people dancing. There I was, unknown to all, even
the police, until the time came to step out again.'
Courage and love won the day. Hearts and homes
which were closed to preaching opened wide to loving
ministry. With her nursing knowledge, Nesta
became in constant demand for confinements,
medical provision being dreadfully lacking in this
respect. A month spent in a home and down would
go the barriers. Several became open converts,
although not in sufficient numbers to form a church
yet ; while others who did not take so definite a
step became her fast friends.

A Gospel car equipped with loud speaker was put
on the road. Within two months Jack Thomas, a
later-joined Crusader with car experience, had
driven it 2,500 miles, sold 2,000 portions of Scripture, besides distributing 5,000 free tracts. He
calculated that 50,000 people must have heard the
messages. It was dangerous work. ' There were
eight attempts on our lives within about ten
days. Here was one. We came to Tuta, snugly
recessed at the foot of a high range. The market
was packed with people. We lifted our hearts in
prayer to the Lord and commenced our meeting.
In a few moments hundreds had gathered round the
car. We had just concluded our message and were
offering our literature for sale. Suddenly a man,
evidently the ringleader, shouted at the top of his

voice, "Down with the Protestants! Kill them. Stone them out of the town. See to it they don't escape alive!" In a flash all the people, with the exception of one old man who is a believer, turned on us.

'The whole town was in an uproar. Women were shrieking, curses flowing freely from every lip. Men and boys were brandishing sticks and stones. Not a few threatened us with knives. The old man stood firmly on our side and shouted at the top of his voice, "These men are true Christian gentlemen and have come to us with the true message of God." But the people cried him down. Stones started to fly thick and fast. I turned and made for the driving cab. There were wild yells. They heard the engine running. With a crash six big stones came hurtling through the windscreen. Glass was flying over my head and shoulders. I decided to drive right ahead. The men leapt aside and at the same time rushed the doors. But, when designing the car, I had the builders fix the door handles so that they could not be opened from the outside. Just as the car was getting clear a big stone came through the side window and caught me on the head, and for a few seconds I was completely dazed. One could only trust the Lord to give what strength was needed. Vaguely I saw the main street ahead, so I steered for it. One hefty man picked up a huge stone, weighing about 50 lbs., and threw it at the engine. His strength was barely sufficient to throw it, but it only bent the engine cover and put a dent in the guard. What a relief to see the open country ahead. . . .'

After several such journeys the Crusaders came to the conclusion that the time was not ripe for such a dramatic approach in the remote villages, where fanaticism is at its strongest. So after a time the car was sold. These long journeys brought us into touch with two busy little towns on the river Magdalena, where the response was eager. Here we have opened stations, at Honda and Giradot. Jack Thomas at Honda has sixty to the meetings, including leading men of the town. There have been several conversions and soon a church will be formed. Bill Easton at Giradot has taken over a work started by the Presbyterians, at their request, and has a congregation of about forty, some of whom help in taking the Gospel to the suburbs and surrounding villages. Here also an indigenous church is in process of formation.

A final example of what prayer and endless persistence can accomplish may be seen from the story of Chiquinquira, the centre of Virgin worship in Colombia, where the cathedral dedicated to her is visited by 250,000 pilgrims in one week. John Harbeson began to work there in 1934. He had the usual experiences of insults, threats with knives, and a period when persecution took the form of obtaining blood from the slaughter-house, smearing it on the door and pouring buckets of it into the house. No one dared come to the meeting-room, but John knows how to attack the Devil, both on his knees and on his feet. With his powerful voice he stood at the door of his empty meeting-room and preached his sermons to the street.

Many would have sought an easier district as years passed and hearts seemed like stone. Only one touch of encouragement had been his, when in his first year he took two souls by faith before the year ended, and two young men came separately to find the way of salvation. The word of the Lord is the hammer that breaks the rock in pieces. He was to find that hungry hearts were drinking in the message behind curtains and open windows. The attitude of many local residents became increasingly friendly. On one or two occasions he passed by houses where he could see the occupants sitting and reading the Bible. The open evidence of the work of the Spirit came in 1938, when, through weekly visits to the gaol, (so far) not the prisoners, but the gaoler, his two elderly sisters and two other members of their family, which has influential connections in the city, publicly confessed Christ and were ex-communicated by name in the Catholic cathedral. To-day there is a little church of some nine members and several adherents. John has used the method of answering controversy simply by opening his Bible and reading the Scriptures. Thus these converts are notably Bible Christians. When an address is given at the meeting, at each quotation from God's Word they insist on looking it up and reading it for themselves. John regards this as a mere beginning. He looks to see a vigorous church, meeting in its own building in the city, and groups of believers in each of the thirteen villages.

We must leave Colombia : 1933 saw the establishment of the work by Pat Symes with his declaration of faith ; 1939 has witnessed the sailing of the fortieth out of the fifty, with two to go, leaving eight to complete the number. Seven of these are associates. Two, Sidney and Ruth McLeod-Jones, from New Zealand, have started an orphanage for the tremendous need of the children wandering homeless by the thousand in the cities, offspring of the terribly immoral conditions in which the people live. The other five are the first missionaries of the Calvary Holiness Church, who have gone out in fellowship with us and spent their first months on our stations until they travelled north to open work in the unevangelized province of Magdalena.

CHAPTER VII

MOUSE CHALLENGES LION

ALEC and Dora Thorne were 'up and down' missionaries, a condition known to many of us ! They were independent workers in another country, 'sometimes conquering, sometimes defeated.' Near them were two women who stressed the Spirit-filled life, 'and I was forced to recognize (wrote Mr. Thorne) that they had a power in their lives more like the power I longed for ; although when one of them had a talk with me on this matter I quickly shut her up.' Yet, on a visit to England, at the Emmanuel Missionary Conference, Birkenhead, he could resist the movings of the Spirit no longer. Although a speaker at the conference, he came forward and knelt at the penitent form, seeking holiness. He arose to live a new life, 'realizing in actual experience, not merely "positionally," that I live, yet not I, but Christ liveth in me.' Mrs. Thorne reached her crisis at a half-night of prayer, after fighting out the battle 'whether I was willing to let God take first place in my husband's life, and be content to take second.' At the meeting she prayed in secret, 'O Lord, grant that I may not have to get up from kneeling here until you have given me the Holy Spirit.' 'I knelt on and prayed on, and before I rose from my knees a deep peace had taken possession of me. Do you think this experience has made

any difference in my life ? Ask my husband. He
has to live with me ! ' At the same conference they
both heard the call to West Africa and joined the
Crusade as members of the fifteen.

By this means the Okak tribe of Spanish Guinea
has received its first missionaries.

Over a course of years I had been searching into
the unevangelized areas of the world, helped particularly by the surveys of the World Dominion
Movement. My attention was early drawn to West
Africa. Throughout its 3,000 miles sweep, from
Mauretania to the Cameroons, I found but a scattered force of missionaries. Some colonies, mainly
British, had a good proportion of occupation. In
the much larger French possessions there was only
a thin line of pioneers ; in the Portuguese colony
none ; and in the Spanish colony we thought none,
but were later to find a recent re-occupation.

Since the Lord had shown us the secret of advance
by faith we had made it our policy that, whenever
an adequate unevangelized field was brought to our
notice, we were bound to accept it as our responsibility. So with West Africa. It appeared to us
that new missionary effort was necessary in Senegal,
Portuguese Guinea, Liberia, Northern Gold Coast,
Ivory Coast, Dahomey and Spanish Guinea. Therefore we hung a map of Africa on the walls of our
prayer room in 1932, indicated these countries by
arrows, and spread them before the Lord, waiting
for Him to give us suitable pioneers for each.

We should consider that we had been breaking the

laws of faith if we had racked our brains to find suitable people, or stretched out a finger to invite anybody. We were careful to occupy ourselves only in receiving them from God, making known the call of West Africa, and daily thanking Him for the prospect of their coming. In six years the wonderful answer, put in a nutshell, has been the outgoing of thirty-five workers and eleven getting ready to sail. Missions have been established in four of these lands ; a fifth is now being started, and Crusaders are preparing to go to the other two.

The Thornes, with their call to Spanish Guinea, were the first volunteers in this West African ' army.' Some months were spent by them at our London headquarters, and the realities of the way of faith seen in a new light. They were to have plenty of chances to put them into action. A few weeks before they sailed, we received information from a reliable source that it was useless to send missionaries to a Spanish colony, as recent laws forbade the entry of missionaries unless of Spanish nationality. It was a heavy blow, and I have to confess that my faith staggered. Other lands were open in West Africa, why should they not go to one of them ? I put it to the Thornes. They went and prayed, but returned to say that God had again spoken clearly and asked them what they were doing considering another country when He had said Spanish Guinea. It took me a week-end to agree to going forward against the laws of a Government ; a week-end of darkness, which only lifted when I heard God saying the same thing to me, recognized His voice and yielded. He had said Spanish Guinea ; very well, if a Government said no, it was a chance for a trial of strength between a temporal power and God, worthy of Bible days.

The Thornes reached the coast of this unknown  little land to find no one on the beach to oppose their entry. A fortnight later the critical moment arrived when they had to visit the governor and present their passports. 'The governor greeted me in a friendly but not enthusiastic style, gave the merest glance at my passport, and said, " Oh, you are a missionary." He did not say anything at all to oppose our going in ; in fact, when I told him we did not know where we should settle down, he said that was all right and that when I let him know he would do what he could for us.' The Lord Jesus had said that the man of prayer is ' shameless ' in his requests (Luke xi. 8, Gr.), and Mr. Thorne acted upon this. He had asked the Lord to make the governor not merely agreeable, but positively helpful. So, ' as he had not yet given the help I was expecting, I said, " May I ask, could you give me any idea as to where would be the most likely parts for me to find the people we want ? " And then he told me the best ways to investigate the land, describing three routes.' The governor himself became their first guide into the interior !

They received many kindnesses from the missionaries of the Southern Presbyterians of U.S.A., at work in the northern half of the colony. They had been in the country many years ago, before the new Spanish laws were promulgated, and on their recent re-entry they were granted special privileges.

Alec Thorne, therefore, was able to concentrate on the southern half of the colony, and made several journeys of investigation in search of the best centre among the Okaks, the largest tribe in the south. In his ignorance of methods of building in the tropics or choice of a suitable site, he made another unusual request to God—for a ready-made mission station. ' On the basis of John xv. 16, I am tremblingly putting it on record that I have asked the Father in Jesus' Name, not only to show me where He wants us to live, but to have the house ready. An impossibility. I have been trying for days to pluck up courage to commit it to writing, but now it is done. He must keep His Word.'

Weeks followed. Invitations were received from various villages, but no offer of a house, so he turned them down. The test became fiercer, as the hut of which they had a temporary loan from a trader was unexpectedly needed by him. ' We have to go from here, and where we are to go I have not the faintest idea. That God will guide us I have no doubt.'

Two days later an invitation came from a town three days away, called Akurenan. Mr. Thorne visited it, both he and Mrs. Thorne being impressed

that this was the place of God's choice. He returned
to say that it was suitable, but ' there was nothing
that could possibly be taken as the Lord's guidance.'
However, so confident were they that the guidance
was coming that they ' prepared the things for shift-
ing.' Mr. Thorne went another ten-day trek, which
included Akurenan on the return journey. This
time the whole aspect of affairs was changed. ' I
heard that the one white man who lives at a shop
here is going to Spain in a hurry because of his
daughter's death.' It turned out that he was glad
to sell the place for a mere song, ' and it was only
finished last December.' Within a few days they had
entered into possession of the house, including a shop
which was later turned into a meeting-room, three
native houses and a large garden well planted with
fruit. ' Our hearts are filled with praises to our
loving Father (he wrote). In all probability I should
never have asked for the seal of a house ready for us
if I had known beforehand how things are done
here, for of course no one ever thinks of doing anything except build their own house, except evidently
fools of faith missionaries ! '

The journey to Akurenan was full of interest.
' The people had many shocks to their nervous
system (wrote Mrs. Thorne) as they saw a white
woman. Before we reached each town one of the
carriers chanted out, " Come and see the white
woman who is going to live at Akurenan." And
the people came.'

On arrival, ' Alec and I went into the house first

68

and thanked the Lord for His goodness. Come with me down the narrow path through the garden, with forest on either side. Down we go, sliding, slithering, but look now in front of you at the lovely clear stream among the iron rocks. This is our private water supply, so clear, so clean that it need not be boiled. Now we will cross over the stream a little way, and—do just look at this—a beautiful little natural pool of clear, cold water, surrounded by rocks of reddish hue and hundreds of tiny ferns. A veritable fairy land, with the trees meeting over-head. I guess the W.E.C.-ers will be found wander-ing there and meeting God in His garden. Above the birds sing and the butterflies hover around, and one feels the beauty of God who made this wonder-ful spot in the forest land.'

They started a little meeting at once, with an audience of thirty, having gained some smatterings of the language from the study of a tribal tongue belonging to the same language group, used by the Presbyterians in the northern half of the colony. A work of God's Spirit was evident from the beginning. Within two weeks ' eight people stayed behind who wished to become " people of God." I asked about fetish medicine, and, oh, the joy of hearing one woman's answer, " Fetish medicine I have not, but I have got a heart filled full of dirt." ' Another week passed and ' another five started on the way of life. One man brought a second lot of fetish medi-cine and said that he had now given up all, and had cut down his tobacco plants and given up tobacco

altogether, and that without any but casual refer-
ences to tobacco.'

Two months after the first meeting Mr. Thorne
writes, 'To His glory I would record that to-day
saw the fiftieth person make a definite profession of
faith in Jesus. I know a couple of these proved un-
satisfactory, but God only knows how many of them
have stretched out a feeble hand of faith to Him, and
" as many as touched Him were made whole." The
fifty come from sixteen different towns.'

The Thornes were joined by two reinforcements,
Lizzie Smith and Emma Munn, neither of whom met
with difficulty on landing. Meanwhile Alec Thorne
began to move out on evangelistic treks, during one
of which 132 made profession of faith. The work
on the station began to go deeper among the
believers and a hunger for holiness of life became
manifest among some. During personal interviews,
after a break in a morning meeting, one believer
said, ' I want to follow the Lord. I was living an
immoral life, but since I had a talk with you I have
not sinned that way. But my trouble is, when I see
an attractive young woman, how can I get rid of the
dirt in my heart ? ' Another said, ' I have hatred in
my heart towards some women in my village ; how
can I get rid of it ? ' ' I believe (wrote Mr. Thorne)
that several sought true heart-cleansing and the
indwelling Holy Spirit.'

Then came the great trial of strength. One day
a Spanish official called Mr. Thorne to his office and
showed him printed orders that missions may not

function unless authorized from Madrid and conducted by Spaniards. 'The official sarcastically told me that, if I was sure God wants us here and would answer my prayers, I could just pray that a special order shall come from Madrid saying that we can work here ; but till that time arrives we are not to be allowed to do so. He said, "Pray that the law of Spain may be changed." I said, " God is all powerful and can do even that." He agreed, but said I have a faith which is " fantastic." '

The test became fiercer when, ten months after their arrival at Akurenan, the order came from the governor that they must report at the capital and live there. The sad journey of 150 miles was taken, ' people coming by the dozen and expressing their sorrow at our going. Poor wee lambs. They tug at our heart-strings.' A whole year was spent in silence, five months at the coast, and the last seven months back at Akurenan whither the governor gave them permission to return, ' on the strict understanding that no mission work was done.' They received a wonderful welcome, ' Possibly 300 have been to see us to-day. The native soldiers, too, have been along to say how glad they are to see us back. One woman believer came in, and as she knew that we could not yet tell her the Words of God, she told them us by repeating all the passages of Scripture she had learned months before.'

Much time was spent in language study and much in prayer, till a day of crisis was reached, although only recognizable to those who understand the

71

secrets of the heavenlies. Each of the four wrote independently to say that God had given them full assurance that deliverance was at hand. Lizzie Smith wrote, for instance, ' God poured light and assurance into my soul that His work would again be resumed.' Mr. Thorne wrote to say how God had brought him back to that interview with the official, when he had stated that God could change the Spanish constitution. ' Now God asked me, '' Can God ? Are you willing to believe for a miracle to be done now and get it by faith ? '' So I prayed definitely that He would do it in His way and have declared my faith in writing.' To the governor-general himself he made the same declaration when he was passing through Akurenan. ' I told him that while I wished to show him all possible respect, I still trusted (in answer to prayer) our request would be granted, for we had come at God's orders.'

In August, just a year after the ban, the expected happened, but in a most unexpected fashion. ' A knock came at the door. Some native soldiers stood there with a letter. It was an official declaration that a state of war was declared and demanded our urgent attendance.' It was their first news of the Spanish revolution. Under an armed escort they were marched to the, capital, and it seemed certain that every hope had now gone. The Roman Catholic priests had already been arrested and deported.

Mr. Thorne wrote : ' I was escorted to the Commandant's house, where he told me it was all right, we were foreigners. While they did not *wish* to have

foreigners in their colony, those who desired to come
would be accorded every facility for normal transac-
tions, but they asked that we should help them in
seeking to keep the natives as calm as possible ; so
would we please immediately return to Akurenan ! '
Certainly they would, and they would get out into
all the villages of their district to ensure the peace-
fulness of their populations by bringing them the
teachings of the Prince of Peace ! The Government
acquiesced, the prayer battle had been won and the
walls of Jericho had fallen ! In a few days the doors
of the meeting-room were open once again, nor have
they since been closed in the two-and-half years from
that date. So far from hindering, the Government
have been pronouncedly helpful, both by the friendliness of local officials and the permit from the central
authorities to build a church.

On November 15, 1936, the outward church of
the Okaks was formed on New Testament lines by
the first baptismal service, ' when thirteen were
received into the visible church and then united in
partaking of the Lord's Supper. Their ages varied
from a lad of about nineteen to old people whose
race on earth is nearly run, wrinkled faces, hair going
white, but joy written on their faces as the windows
of their hearts. Afterwards there must have been
joy in the heart of the Lord as He saw some of the
gifts they put in the box placed on the table, the first
time any such thing had been done. A spirit of quiet
and holy joy, yet of great solemnity, pervaded the
whole. It is a thing that can seldom fall to the

73

lot of a person to see the founding of the visible
church in a previously unreached part ; and words
fail to express the joy it means.' This first church
has now risen to sixty in number. They have been
carefully educated in their responsibilities as church
members to recognize the Holy Spirit, and not the
white missionary, as their Lord. They have learned
to judge sin in their midst, to be a witnessing church,
as is evidenced by their increase, and have elected
their own elders, women as well as men.

The conflicts of these years have taken toll of the
little band of pioneers. Both Lizzie Smith and Mrs.
Thorne had to return home, although Mrs. Thorne
has now been able to rejoin her husband. Eighteen
months ago Mr. Thorne himself was told by the
doctor that he risked his life if he stayed out a further
six months ; but rather than let the work collapse, as
it might well have done from the official standpoint
if the only man had returned home, he remained on
at risk of life. Emma Munn also has been seriously
ill, but has risen again from her sick bed to spend
two periods of six weeks and four months alone in a
large village four days from Akurenan, where the
head man and his people had begged for a teacher.

' God has given me the joy of leading many souls
to Jesus (she wrote). After each meeting those who
wanted to get right with God would come to my
house. One came asking if he could be forgiven the
sin of eating a man. Some had made a previous
profession and fallen, adultery being the chief cause.
Another confessed to being a witch-doctor. One

woman followed me into the house with a native
tray full of bananas. I thanked her for them, but she
simply stood there and not a word was uttered. Then
she said, " I have eaten people, I have committed
adultery, I have lied, I have done all kinds of evil
things." I said to her, " Do you want God to forgive your sins and make you a new creature ? "
What a look of relief came into her eyes as she said,
" Yes, I do." Thank God for the privilege of leading
her to Jesus.'

This woman became the first to reveal the secret
fetish of those villages. She took Miss Munn to her
hut in the forest, slid open a secret panel inside
which was a long dark passage. ' She pointed and
said, " They're in there." I went in, wondering
what I should find. I could only see a dirty square
box. I brought it out. " Is that it ? " " Yes, pass
me quickly." As I took it home I met one of the
women believers. When she saw my load, she let
out a yell and ran across the forest. By this time I
was getting more curious and hurried home. When
I had shut the door, I opened the box and discovered
—just two human skulls. Pedro, the head man,
told me that when they want to do witchcraft, they
take down a skull and tell it the person they want
to kill. " They pray to it just as we do to God." '

Miss Munn found that the believers treasured the
memory of the few texts and choruses taught them,
and passed them on to others. On each visit she
taught them to memorise more. On her most recent
visit she found a church built, a house for herself

and the people regularly at worship, so that we may say that the second church of the Okaks has now been founded at Chief Pedro's. The first book of texts in the Okak language has now been sent to England to the Scripture Gift Mission, who have kindly consented to print it, so that the people may have some part of the Word of God in their own language.

CHAPTER VIII

NO LIMITS TO GOD

WITH the completion of the ten and the fifteen, we published a leaflet with the title 'Faith is Substance.' In the last paragraph we wrote, ' The glory to us is the knowledge that God has given us access to Himself in pleading the needs of the unevangelized world and the necessity of occupying every still unoccupied region. We know as plainly as we can know that He has opened to us His treasure house for this purpose, and is expecting us to draw on Him increasingly without regard to world conditions of distress and depression round us. Next year it is to be " The Story of the Twenty-five," for we are going to ask Him for another twenty-five workers before the third anniversary of Mr. Studd's death, July 16, 1934.'

In our daily meetings we had the usual feelings of the foolishness of faith ! One day in November we were laughing at the absurdity of our little group sitting there and talking of receiving £3,250 in the next eight months, specifically given for new missionaries. For some reason, we even discussed in what sums we would like the money to come, and decided that we would ask God for three £1,000 gifts and one of £250. I do not say that there was any particular sense or meaning in making such a request. Still there it is, we did so ; and I have learned to realize that the more we exercise all the liberty of children with our Heavenly Father, the more it pleases His loving heart.

We seemed to get what we did not ask more quickly than what we did ask. We had not asked for candidates, for we knew that they would come forward all right, and by December there were eight for certain and an assurance of another ten ready by the end of the year. Eighteen applicants—but only £20.

A few days later a woman was ushered into the sitting-room. She was from the midlands and a friend of the work. We thought that she had come just on a visit, but after a minute or two she told us that a sum of money had unexpectedly come to her and that she wished to put it in our hands for advance work in unevangelized fields. It was, she thought, £1,000. The cheque arrived in January. It was for £1,011. The first £1,000.

The next day there arrived a letter from the west of England. In it was a promise of £1,000 towards the outgoing of some of the candidates for the fields. The second £1,000 in two days.[1]

A month later we had a short letter on an ordinary sheet of paper torn from a writing pad asking for further information about the Crusade. Our reply was followed by another letter, asking to whom a donation should be addressed. As it had no particular

[1] Actually, only a small portion of this £1,000 was ultimately received, because it was conditional on there being a need for it, and, owing to new equipping facilities, we were able to reduce costs considerably, and these were chiefly covered by the other gifts.

78

letter-head or anything impressive about it, our minds turned to, perhaps, a £10 gift. A third letter followed with a cheque inside. As the figures at the bottom were a bit smudged, we had to look at the line of writing above. It was ' One Thousand Pounds ' for new fields. The third £1,000.

The very next day from the other end of the country came a cheque for £250 ' for advance work.' The £3,250 in four gifts within three months. By the Father's wonderful bounty our thoughts were turned from the need of money to the need of candidates. Yet all were in by July 16, and after being tested they went to the different fields. Thirteen men and twelve women to six fields.

Meanwhile we were also learning in London something more of the truth of the first word in the promise, ' *Whatsoever* ye shall ask in My Name, that will I do.'

With the growth of the headquarters, all kinds of new workers were needed, often with specialized knowledge, and for each a miracle was necessary, for not only must the person be found who had the necessary experience, but in each case they must have a call to live by faith, receiving nothing from Mission funds.

One of the first was my need of a secretary, trained as a stenographer. No steps were taken to find one beyond the usual—a transaction with God in the prayer room ; but the Lord had the answer ready before the call. There was a woman, Miss Elizabeth Hand, whom I had met twice at a conference, whose

name I had forgotten, nor did I know her profession. As a matter of fact, she was working in the
Ministry of Pensions and living in London. For
some years the Lord had given her a longing to
spend the rest of her life in His service, and she was
much drawn to the W.E.C. With her experience as
a stenographer she wanted to offer her gifts to Him.
Unknown to me, a mutual friend from our inner
circle mentioned our prayer to her. She offered for
the position. I explained to her what it would mean
to live with no earthly means of support behind her,
after she had been accustomed for years to a salary.
She prayed over it, wrote again to say that God
was calling her and that she had resigned her
position.

The proof that a call is from God is that it stands
the test in the furnace. So with this one. A fortnight after she had given notice, Miss Hand received
papers from the Ministry of Pensions which, when
filled up, would mean that she would be put on the
list of those entitled to a pension. She had to choose
between continuing her employment with a life's
pension in view, or losing all earthly prospects of
support for present and future. She did not waver,
and for six years has been a mother in Israel among
us, now finding her sphere not merely in secretarial
work, but as head over the young women, and hostess
of the New Hostel.

Then came the need of more room. We had overflowed from No. 17 to No. 19, and were still expand-
ing. It was obvious what to ask for—another house,

and the one we wanted was obvious also, for the house exactly opposite, No. 34, was up for sale. Again, response to the Lord's call was accompanied by the sacrifice which glorifies Him, the proof that only love for Him could have inspired such an action. Miss Lilian Gristwood had a lovely house in Edgbaston, Birmingham. Her father had just passed away, and she had re-decorated the house and partly re-furnished it in modern style. God 'called' and she gave up all to buy No. 34 for use as a W.E.C. guest-house. Neither house, garden nor situation were anything like so attractive as her Birmingham home. For five years she was herself the house-mother, till her health made it necessary to take a flat nearby, the house still remaining as part of the headquarters.

Again there was the practical side of things. I had the vision of an equipment store from which we could provide the equipment for outgoing missionaries at wholesale prices. There was also the oversight of the men candidates, repairs and alterations in the mission houses which they might undertake, a hundred and one ways in which the Lord's money could be saved if we had the right overseer. Within a few months of our beginning to pray for such a person the Lord sent him, equipped in each one of these separate ways ! Leslie Sutton had been with Mr. Studd in Congo until invalided home through the effects of a war wound, so he knew what was needed for candidates. He was the practical man *par excellence*, having heard the call as a lad and prepared himself in carpentering, building, cooking, medicine and other ways, so that he could take the oversight of the houses. He had spent a period in business where he had gained experience in wholesale buying, just right for the equipment store ! Jehovah-Jireh, the Lord the Provider !

Under ' Suto's ' hands the practical side of head-quarters was revolutionized. ' The Stables,' No. 19, of which the coachman's flat had long been a ser-viceable set of four-roomed offices, now had the old coach-room turned into an equipment store, the hay loft into a men's dormitory with eight beds, ship's bunk fashion, the horse stalls into a bath-room and workshop, the space for washing the coaches into a garage ! In the equipment alone a saving of nearly 40 per cent has been effected. The description of the greatest triumph, the building of the New Hostel, is reserved for a later chapter.

So the story goes on. Like the writer to the Hebrews, time fails me to tell of all the Lord has done. Outstanding has been the gift of beloved Jock Purves, best known of all Crusaders in the British Isles. Himself in earlier days a Crusader in Lesser Tibet, the Lord recalled him from going into the ministry, where he would have had much acceptance as a preacher with the gift of Scottish eloquence, to the very much more humble and costly life of show-ing men and women up and down the country how we can take up our cross for Christ and an unevan-gelized world at home. Through him many have seen a new thing—that they can be Crusaders at home as much as on the fields ; that a business man or housewife can leave all and follow Christ in their daily lives ; that they can know the adventure and exploits of a life of faith, as thoroughly as those called to what we wrongly term 'full-time service.' Financing and filling public meetings, starting prayer batteries which become recruiting grounds for the front lines, turning homes into local Crusade headquarters, arranging conferences by faith, turning parts of holidays into W.E.C. treks, these are some of their activities, while the full tale of all the self-denial and prayer which forms the hidden background of the Crusade will never be told till the Day reveals it.

Others that the Lord has sent are each a story in themselves and each fills a special niche. Olive Ashton, over from the Canadian H.Q., is our conference organiser. Fred Lyons, who now relieves Leslie Sutton in the practical work, left his father's farm in Ireland, while his sister, Annie, moves about taking meetings. Fred Anthony, who could get a position anywhere as private secretary, shares my work. Mrs. Purves, now hostess of No. 34, is in charge of the catering of the whole household. John Whittle has left a church to do advance work in towns where the Crusade is not known. Ena Bush left an assured position in the head office of an overseas bank to fulfil another vision, the starting of a young people's Crusade on lines that appeal to youngsters. They are called ' The Young Warriors.' They have their ' palavers,' with testimonies, singing and prayer by themselves. Each band has a front-line warrior, for whom they pray and work. They have their own special countersign and war cry, copied from the Christians of the Congo.

Yet others are called to share in the headquarters work in special ways, though carrying on in their own professions. Outstanding among these is Charlton Smith. As an artist and designer he has r volutionized our publications. His vision is that the Lord ought to have the best that modern methods can produce, with the result that under the new title *World Conquest* he has made our magazine as up-to-date as any modern publication, to fit the most up-to-date message the world can ever hear—the Gospel of Christ. It costs him hours, gladly given late at nights, designing and drawing maps, covers, sketches, lay-outs. Yet another is Phil Dyer, who at his home has fitted up all the photographic equip-ment necessary for printing, enlarging and slide-making, and is able to turn out the many slides we need at a quarter the usual cost. We can well say with the Psalmist, How manifold are Thy works, O Lord.

CHAPTER IX

THE LAME TAKE THE PREY

I REMEMBER meeting S. J. Staniford at the
station in 1932, and, as he was led along like a
blind man, thinking to myself, ' There's the end of
a fine life.' He had been fourteen years in the Congo,
and since Mr. Studd's death was assistant leader.
He had built up a church of a thousand members at
Wamba, when his missionary career seemed to close
down by the growth of cataracts on both eyes, most
unusual for a man in the early forties. There was
nothing for it but to return to London for the
operation. It was successful, but of course the sight
could never be the same again.

The future for him seemed very uncertain until
the W.E.C. conference at Swansea that year. There
the heavens opened on all and we saw the reality of
those words, ' Greater works than these shall ye do,
because I go unto My Father.' There also God
spoke to ' Sta ' and his wife on the conditions essential to seeing these greater works happen. An
adjustment needed to be made, a point in their personal lives where, with middle age coming on, they
had begun to substitute reliance on man for naked
trust in God ; and those who do that in the least
degree can neither see nor obey the heavenly vision
which demands the hazarding of all for its fulfilment.

85

There *was* a purpose in their home-coming—a far greater purpose than a return to Wamba. Something which might never have been fulfilled if he had remained a fit man and not been caused, thanks to his affliction, to wonder what he could do in the future ; and equally something which might never have dawned on him as a possibility if he had not plunged again into 'living dangerously.' West Africa came before them. There was need enough in Congo, but at least the church of Christ had begun to take shape there : whereas in Ivory Coast and adjacent lands the names of fifteen large tribes were known who had never had a witness to Christ. Could such as he go there with his dimmed eyesight ? Why not ? His fifteen years' experience of native work was more valuable than perfect natural sight.

He talked with us and we rejoiced. This was of all things what we needed. A man with ripe missionary experience, and, above all, one who had worked long with C. T. Studd and who could introduce into our West African field—which we already saw in vision stretching over 2,000 miles and seven lands—all the best that had been learned with the old warrior in the Congo. It was a sacrifice for the Congo field, but they gladly made it, that they might thus stretch out their stakes to the West Coast.

Preparations were at once put in hand, and Mr. Staniford sailed in November, 1934, accompanied by Fred Chapman. For some months previously he had been asking the Lord for a car, built to his own specification, as he knew the type best suited to the country and had heard of the magnificent French Colonial roads. On September 27 the Lord distinctly said to him, ' I will give you a car to-morrow.' So certain was he of the Lord's voice that he told a friend. To-morrow came and no sign of a car. A few days previously he had given a farewell message at our London annual meeting and, I need hardly add, had not mentioned his secret prayer. A woman from the north was present. She had not been able to attend the annuals for years, but happened to be in London that day. She wrote to me, saying that she was particularly impressed with Sta's talk and asking more about him. I was away, and so her letter did not get answered for a few days. A further letter then came, saying that she would like to help Sta by the gift of a car. He was thrilled with the news and told me of the assurance he had received, but the date was a puzzle, for he was sure the Lord had said the 28th. It occurred to me to look up the first letter I had received from the lady and there we found the solution. It was dated September 28 !

The two took the car with them and thus were able, on landing at the coast, to motor inland and make a thorough tour of investigation before deciding on the area in which to start work. Sta had seen and learned the way in which the Lord will distinctly speak to those who wait on Him.

IVORY COAST

87

They were not attempting, therefore, to make their choice by the mere study of maps or inquiry from officials ; but rather they motored from place to place, learning all they could, but leaving the ultimate decision to a clear leading from the Spirit. This was especially necessary in their case, because the French Government were cautious in granting permits for missionary work ; an application had to carry with it the approval of the local official before the central authorities would grant it, and cases had been known where missionaries, although allowed in the country, had moved from place to place unable to obtain local sanction.

Sta seemed destined to a like fate. During his first tour of 300 miles he found the tribe of God's choosing. ' We made contact with the Gouro tribe, who have Bouaflé as their centre. We find that there are about 115,000 of them, but no mission work of any kind among them, and we take it that the Lord would have us enter there.' With the guidance clear, application was made to the governor through the local administrator for permission to work among them. ' Now we are settling down to praying this Bouaflé official " through " as concerns this permission.'

But once again, as with the car, something seemed to have gone wrong with the guidance. The official was not at all favourable. ' He proceeded to try to scare us ! The Gouros would never be converted as they are so attached to fetishism. This was a centre of poisoning. If there is an idol at the entrance of the village and you ignore it, most likely any water you drink will be poisoned. If we began to attack or ridicule fetishism he would not be at all responsible for what might happen. The only way to get converts would be to have a soldier over them with a bayonet, for only on fear of death would they change. And so on!' No wonder that a month later, in March, 1935, we had a letter from Sta saying, 'The old enemy is doing his level best to win the game, but we are not throwing up the sponge yet. On Thursday the long-awaited reply of the governor arrived, saying, "I regret to inform you that I cannot grant the permission asked for." That was a great shock and surprise. We both felt assured right from the time we applied that permission would be granted. We cannot understand why the Lord has allowed this to happen. It drives us back to His leading and seals on our coming here, and we have to say that we know *He* sent us. So we are waiting for Him to open His door for us.'

Another journey of 500 miles into the interior was taken, several centres being touched. One, Vavoua, they discovered to be at the cross-roads leading to several tribes, and including the northern edge of the Gouros. 'Vavoua will be a splendid place for us to begin work. From there we could branch west to the Toura and Mahou people, north to the Senoufous, and east to the Gouros. At Vavoua there are about 12,000 Gouros. To-morrow I hope to get off again to Vavoua and make contact with the officials. If we find them friendly we shall take that as an indication that the Lord is opening that door. It will be a great day when we have permission to go full steam ahead, and it will come. I have felt the Lord saying to me that this is the last trip in the search for this first place in Ivory Coast.'

He arrived at Vavoua to find the door wide open. ' The first news we heard was that the Administrator had left, and in his place the Lord brought in a new one who has never before served in Ivory Coast, whose attitude towards us is most kind and sympathetic. A few weeks later he told us that he could give us good hope of obtaining the permission, as he had reported favourably, because he felt that we should work for the true well-being of the natives, in full loyalty to the French Administration.'

A few days later came this letter—' The Lord has done great things for us whereof we are glad. In fact we have been dancing for joy. A quarter of an hour ago a native messenger brought the governor's letter, which runs as follows, " . . . I authorize you to evangelize the cantons of the Gouros, Kouyas, Nedibouas of the sub-division of Vavoua." '

What they did not realize at the time was that the closing of Bouaflé in the south and the opening of Vavoua at the northern end of the tribe, after three refusals and nine long months of waiting, far from being a set-back, was actually God's way of giving them the whole tribe according to His promise. Relations between the missionaries and the French officials became increasingly cordial, especially with one official in the Vavoua area. In 1938, Mr. Staniford was led to re-apply for permission to work among the southern Gouros round Bouaflé. No sooner had he sent in his application than the news came that the Government were making an alteration in the administrative districts, that in future the whole of the Gouro tribe were to be under one control, and the man chosen for the position was their special friend ! Through him the Government has given us entry into the forbidden sector which might never otherwise have been given ; the first visits have been paid and two workers are now established at a centre in the Bouaflé district. Without fuss or worry, all that was received from God by faith has come out in substance, and the days are now not far distant when the Father will be glorified in the Son in every village of Gouroland.

This is anticipating. Mrs. Staniford arrived from England the same week as the first permit at Vavoua. We had been praying in London that it would be granted by the time she arrived, and it was signed by the governor on the day she landed, June 3, 1935. The three started life together in a native village. From his experience in the Congo, Mr. Staniford knew that the best response to the message is in the villages where civilization has not yet penetrated. It had been customary for the French only to grant permission for a mission station to be built close to an official centre, but Sta boldly asked that he might build on a site two miles out. The request was granted ; he believed at the time that it was the first permit given to a mission for a rural concession, although he has since learned of two others. They began their life in village huts until the first mission house, built by themselves, became habitable, in a healthy situation on a slight rise near the village. Fred Chapman describes their early contacts with the Gouros. ' Having learned that a village off the main road was the place of the paramount chief, we decided to visit it. The track ran for seven miles over a marsh—and what a ride ! Our car was like a rocking chair and bucking broncho almost all the way. A crowd of women curiously watched us as we pulled up in this lonely village. On finding somewhere to spend the night, several young men came to help us in putting our beds inside. We were soon great friends. Tea was made and gratefully we sat down to enjoy it, in spite of the large amount of black clay in it. Being the close of the dry season, there is little water, and this marsh water was particularly filthy. We strolled through the village at sunset. Men and boys were lazily sprawling on beautifully plaited smooth mats, whilst the women and girls prepared plantains and yams. These people are simple, ignorant, raw pagans.

' Next day we arose early for a great feast. The Bread of Life is our most precious possession. As we were busy with our toilet a group gathered round to watch the beautiful white lather being ploughed off our manly jaws ; then, when we extracted our teeth to clean them, what horror ! Some shrieked and unconsciously held in their teeth ! Others were called to see this great thing. Every time we laughed, after this episode, they would stare in expectation of our teeth dropping out ! Later we walked round the village. In an open round shed was the blacksmith. He was tempering a knife and preparing a rough iron spade. His assistant sat in a comfortable position as he rhythmically thrust his fists alternately into air bellows formed of monkey skins. Strolling a little farther we saw heaps of flying ants roasting in the sunshine. They had been caught during the night. It was interesting to watch a woman winnowing the wings from these fat insects. Occasionally she would eat a handful and generously offered me some. I tried several and found them passable. This delighted the old dears standing around, and when I blurted out, " E ya nini ! " (They are good !), their joy overflowed.

' In the evening we had a great time with the chief and elder men, the young men joining in, explaining to them that Christ, the only Son of God, had come to this earth to bring God's thoughts from Heaven. Their appetites were whetted. Then we splashed into the sin problem. The chief asked questions and seemed very interested, saying that he would be very pleased for us to have a house at his village to teach them the things of God's Book. I am certain the Lord has opened the way to these folk.'

Gradually they saw farther into the hopelessness of paganism. ' We had just finished our evening meal. As it was a glorious moonlit night after a blazing hot day, I took my chair outside. Soon after, a young man came straight across the compound and said simply, " He's dead ! He died just now ! " As we were there talking a sudden great noise burst forth. In a few seconds the whole village was filled with a hideous din. People were dashing about and crying like madmen. On arriving near the hut in which was the dead man an amazing sight and noise met us. A hundred or more natives were yelling and shuffling along outside the house. The near relatives were dancing, stamping their feet, lifting their hands in the air and uttering a variety of heathen shrieks. Oh, the terrible hopelessness of these pagan hearts. Women in twos and threes paraded the village. Some were almost nude, some were totally covered in slate-grey mud slime and did sensuous dances as they chanted or shrieked. A group of old men, each one a fetishist, met and sat outside my window. I saw some of the fetishes, and what a filthy collection of rubbish it was ! Thank God that faith in the risen Christ is the victory.'

What a contrast was seen when the angel of death paid another visit to that village seven months later. A little group of mourners, their every movement watched with inquisitive amazement by the villagers, were laying the earthly remains of Lilian Staniford in the grave. The dreaded yellow fever in three days had snatched the life which had resisted the malaria of the Congo for sixteen years. Sorrowfully they laid the precious burden to rest, yet always rejoicing, for the words of the angel spoken at another tomb 2,000 years before echoed down the ages to that African graveside, ' He is not here; He is risen.' That little Gouro group of watchers were the first to see the triumph over death of faith and hope in Christ, which will yet be seen at hundreds of Gouro gravesides in the years to come. The first corn of wheat had fallen into the ground and died to bring forth the Gouro harvest.

Sta was to have the privilege of sharing Christ's cup of suffering for West Africa to an unusual extent. The sudden death of ' Ma Sta ' had been preceded six months earlier by the dimming of the sight of one of his eyes, already so weakened by the operation. A few months later he was involved in a severe motor accident, which left him bleeding at the roadside, with his scalp laid open from the forehead to the nape of the neck. There was no hope of life for him had not ' by chance ' a motorist been passing along the road that hour, who staunched the flow of blood and sent 40 miles for a doctor, who took him next day 120 miles to a hospital. Gradually he recovered, but the accident left him with permanent injury to the drum of one ear. The sight of an eye, the hearing of an ear and his beloved wife taken from him within a year, made us naturally anxious about his condition and we suggested a return to England. He would not hear of it and has adhered to his decision. Sufferings and losses mean to him the fulfilment of the law of harvest. The corn of wheat must die that it may bring forth much fruit.

Six days before the anniversary of their arrival in

95

Ivory Coast the first Gouro confessed Christ. ' After
the evening meal (wrote Fred Chapman) we had one
solitary visitor. We hardly expected the usual crowd
owing to a rain-storm. This young man had shown
signs of more definite interest in the things of God
recently. The Lord told me what to say and I said
it. " Gotta, there's a great difference between you
and us. We have something to live for, to work for,
an aim in life : but what about you ? We have
been born again, because we have been washed
from our sins by Jesus' blood. When will you come
to Jesus for cleansing ? " After a little chat we
prayed. His prayer was jerky and scrappy, but one
sentence was outstandingly clear, " Jesus, I want
you to wash my heart clean." We understand that
he regularly prays before retiring to bed, and for
months has had nothing to do with fetishes.'

Several villages now have believers ; very feeble
in most cases, for none have the written Word and
most have only heard the Gospel on an occasional
visit. Some have put away fetishes and been driven
by fear to return again to them. As best they
know how, they have begun ' to walk the path that
leads to the village of God.' As one put it, ' It's
true what you say. We have lived for filth all our
lives and never thought of anything better till you
came. We can't read and you have the Word of
God. You must tell us what to do.' Here and there
true light has dawned. ' Kwadi has grasped the
fact of the sacrificial death of Jesus for himself. He
was far from attractive, either in features or character,

and I began to think of him as " that ugly fellow."
But a great change has come.' In two villages ' there
are several who meet for prayer.' In another village,
which is near the station and under more constant
teaching, there has been, recently, a real break, the
chief and several with him declaring themselves
for Christ. The missionary staff among the Gouros
has increased to seven. Two more Gouro stations
are being opened. Fred Chapman has reduced the
language to writing and sent home the first book of
texts for printing. With constant watering of the
soil and by preaching the Word there is no doubt
that a few years will see groups of believers throughout the villages of Gouroland.

*   *   *   *   *

We move 500 miles north of the Gouros to the
Lobi tribe and hear a strange and wonderful story.
The first pioneer to go to them was C. S. Benington
of the Qua Iboe Mission. He settled among them
in 1931, having first gained the cautious approval of
the French official, who told him to be ' extremely
careful,' as part of the tribe is still unsubdued. He
made little headway among this idol-worshipping
people until the coming of a drought in 1932. The
head chief then came to ask, ' Are you stopping the
rain?' ' No,' said Mr. Benington, ' but it is God's
way of speaking to you.' A number of the leading
men came to see him, 'suspicious, evil-looking men,
every one with bows and arrows,' while he urged
them to turn to God from idols and prayed for rain.

Still it did not come, until finally the chief came to say, ' The crops are dead.'

Shortly before, Benington had been praying and had received the strange word that the crops would die and that then the Lord would send rain to revive them. So for the last time he told the chief to call the people and made a final appeal, ' Is there a man here who will take the Son of God as his Saviour and throw away his idols?' Then the remarkable happened. Two men came forward.

' The first thing for you to do is to throw away your idols.'

' We haven't got any idols.'

' You must have. I have been all round your village and they are everywhere.'

' Our house is behind the swamp and we have no idols.'

Then one of them told this story. ' Eleven harvests ago I was in my house one night preparing for a great sacrifice. I was to be raised in rank as a witch doctor. The heathen doctors were coming early next morning. I went to sleep. While I slept God came to me and picked me up and threw me over the side of my house. Three times He did that and then called me by name. " You must throw away your idols. The day of idols is passed, because I am going to send a white man and his wife into your village and they will teach you My way." '

' Was it a dream?' asked Benington.

' No, I saw God. Next morning, when I stepped

out and saw my idols, I said, " These are the things God has told me to destroy." I took my axe and smote my chief idol. The witch doctors caught hold of me and said I had gone mad and that it would mean death.'

The persecution continued. They made sacrifices ' to try and drive the madness out of his head,' but God had got hold of him. Then he went round the tribe telling them to throw away their idols and that God had appeared to him. Hundreds of people threw them away.

However, weeks lengthened into months and months into years and they began to say, ' Why doesn't the white man appear ? ' Then they began to take their idols back again. After a few years only two men remained. They had heard the voice of God and were not going to be disappointed. They waited for ten long years and then Mr. Benington came. That day, on the mud floor of the verandah, ' two strong Lobi men prayed that God would take the blood of His Son and wash their hearts and live in their hearts so that they might walk in His way. I don't suppose it was ten minutes afterwards, as I was standing outside, I saw big black clouds come up and presently the rain came crashing down. Next morning the chief came to say, " We know God sent that rain. The crops that were dead yesterday are beginning to turn green. They have risen from the dead." ' God wanted to show them a God that could bring life out of death.

From that remarkable beginning the work steadily

99   G 2

progressed, until by 1937 there were 150 converts, the difficult language was reduced to writing and John's Gospel translated. At this juncture Mr. Benington was recalled by his mission to their Nigerian field. He was already in close touch with Mr. Staniford, for he had long prayed for 100 missionaries for West Africa and believed that the entry of the W.E.C. was part of the answer ; so he was glad to arrange for us to link on the Lobi work with the Gouro, making these two tribes the jumping-off places for entry into another ten tribes in the regions around to which no Gospel witness has yet gone, the Malinkes, Senoufous, Nefagas, Tagouanas, Koulongos and Bonnas ; the Djans, Birifos, Dagaries and Gourounsis.

Jack Robertson, the first W.E.C. volunteer for the Ivory Coast (now joined by his wife and five others), took over the work at Bouroum and has become by prayer and tears and labour an apostle to these 80,000 Lobis, perhaps the toughest pagan tribe we have yet contacted. ' I went to live a few months in a village. I got an insight into their lives ; in fact, I got a bit more than I reckoned, and a few times was shocked, horrified and disgusted at what I saw. In some things they are just like animals. Idols have such a tremendous hold upon them that I feel like changing the name of Lobiland to Idol-land. I went to see one idol room, armed with a good flashlight. What a sight met my eyes ! There they were, dirty, dusty, in pitch darkness and smeared with the blood of sacrifices. They are a poisoned arrow tribe. As they approach they lift the right arm up until the palm of the hand is facing you shoulder high. This means they are not going to put one of their nasty-looking arrows into you. Their dress is of the scantiest. I have seen people strolling about our compound totally naked, adults, not children, although most at least have a string of beads.'

One of their worst customs is the initiation festival, held every seven years. ' The sacred grove lies just behind our house and we are able to hear all the cries they make to the evil spirits. At it the youth of the tribe is taught and made to practise unthinkable vileness. At the end they all marched to the market place, dressed up, the boys with head-dresses of feather and armlets of cowrie shells, the girls with head-dresses and ceintures of cowrie shells. It was a sight to see them. My heart went out in love to these folk desiring them for the Lord Jesus.'

CHAPTER X

TENDERFEET DO IT

TWO young men, with no previous missionary experience, in the heart of a country as large as the British Isles, the only light amid hosts of heathenism ! North of them you could travel 1,200 miles before you reached another missionary witness. East, 1,000 miles. West, towards the ocean, 200 miles, still without the Gospel; and south through another country never yet entered.

It certainly was a risk letting two ' tenderfeet ' go thus into ' the white man's grave.' Strange people, strange food, strange climate. A land where the sun can strike with deadly force, where yellow fever takes its mortal toll in a few days, where wrong foods and unclean water have laid many a strong life low. However, 2,000,000 souls were there and no other volunteer to take them the Gospel. They were willing and eager to go. God had called. Who were we to refrain from giving them the right hand of fellowship and supplying them with all the advice we could give, knowing them to be sane and sensible as well as spiritual young men?

So in 1936 Ted Gibbons and Leslie Brierley set sail for Senegal, the core of a huge unevangelized territory, reaching northward through Mauretania and Rio de Oro, eastward through French Sudan, and southward through Portuguese Guinea and part of French Guinea, and comprising a scattered, mainly desert, population of about 3,000,000, the large majority Moslems who are rapidly engulfing the remaining pagans.

They landed at Dakar and were helped by the only other missionary in the whole vast area, a Frenchman working among the French at the port. On into the interior they pushed their way, all being new and strange to them. Their first experience of African travel was by lorry on a road which when in England they had thought would be ' a fine concrete one.' It turned out to be ' a rough old sandy track with roots of trees sticking out. . . . At about 7 p.m. down came the rain. How it fell ! How the lightning increased ! It was practically incessant and lit up the whole forest. I thought, " This is African rain, is it ? " In less than two minutes we were soaked to the skin, for we had no windscreen. Our main road had become a river. All of a sudden we stopped. " What's the matter ? " I asked the driver. " We have sunk in the mud," he said. Out we had to jump, ankle deep in mud, and in the darkness break down pieces off the trees and ram them under the back wheels of the lorry.'

One more help with which to start their life was the loan of a dilapidated old mission house, once occupied by workers who had left for another country and kindly gave them permission to use it. 'We arrived at midnight, opened the door, made

ourselves some oxo, got down our bed bags and at
1.40 a.m. dropped down on to our mattresses.' Thus
their first night in the heart of Senegal.

They had to get used to all the sounds of Africa,
such as on the next evening when Ted ' went into another room, but retreated again as I heard something
rustling in the straw. In the morning I saw that it
was nothing worse than a large yellow and blue
lizard !

' After a day or two the natives, who had been
looking at us from the fence of the compound,
plucked up courage and came to within what they
felt to be a safe distance to look at the white men.
They all proved very friendly, but as time went on
their friendliness was little more than skin deep, as
they were fanatically Moslem. Having no gramma r,
we began to find out by one means and another from
the natives something of their language. Our time
was occupied with language study, constantly
repairing the house, which was always needing it,
and visiting the village.

' Our garden boy has two speeds—slow and stop
—and he seems to use the lower gear most (wrote
Leslie Brierley). Ted says that the weeds grow
quicker than he moves, so we go round in a circle !
Weeds in Africa are not the tiny things one sees at
home. Some grow three feet high ! We have some
wild flowers in the front part of the garden which
resemble marguerites. One morning I looked out
and there was his lordship rooting up the flowers—
the only flowers we have. Naturally I asked him

to refrain from committing sacrilege like that, in a voice tender but firm ! He looked up quite innocently and said, " You eat them, then ? " He couldn't understand that they should be kept for their beauty. Perhaps it is only when Jesus enters their lives that these folk, who are surrounded with country which is constantly declaring the beauty of God, can see beauty in nature.

' The insects are a real pest. Isaiah calls Africa " The land of the rustling of wings," and so it is. There is a constant buzz, hum and whistle ! We could manage if it were only that, but when they insist on taking liberties and walking all over one's face and arms, biting betimes, it gets rather too much ! One night we had an invasion of aeroplanes —great big insects with four wings apiece and a large amount of cheek. . . .'

After a few months they set out in turn to spy out the land and exercise their small stock of language. Inexperienced in the usual trekking methods, they piled all they could, which was not much, on the back of their cycles instead of having carriers, and might well have been in difficulties if caught by fever. Still the God of the 91st Psalm carried them through, though not without sufferings and hardships. Of the contacts made on such journeys, Leslie Brierley wrote, when on a later trek, ' Early in the morning we were on the move. At 11 a.m. we struck off into the bush. There are here no giant forests, just woodland such as one would see in England. Down went the packs of the porters in

the centre of the village, just near the " parlour " of
the chief, the bamboo seat arrangement which every
African here builds for sitting out during the day.
When the people had finished their evening meal
they gathered there. The seat was full and many
stood round, while I began telling the old, old
Story. Many, if not most, were listening for the
first time to the Gospel. I had planned to stay here
for five nights and to spread the Gospel during that
time. Try to imagine that for the first time you are
listening to such a story, and calculate just how much
you would grasp of its significance at one sitting !
One of the difficulties is to find words to fit our more
abstract terms.

' Next night I spoke on " God is Love." As I
preached the chief said, " We hear your words and
they are sweet. We have work to do to-morrow and
it is late, but we will gladly sit and listen to you yet
awhile, so please go on." How the love of God
attracts. On the last evening, although some had
lost interest and dropped out, quite a few still hung
on every word. This time it was the climax,
Calvary. Many said they believed. Of course it is
easy to get natives to say that, but we do know the
Holy Ghost was working.

' These people are beer drinkers, and because of
this do not desire to become Moslem. It is our
glorious privilege to tell them of Jesus. But that
does not also mean that they appreciate it. Most of
them are politely indifferent, and are not of those
who greedily grasp the Good News. One said, " I

shall continue to drink until I die, my heart is clean
enough ! " But there is plain enough evidence that
with persistent visitation a number in these villages
will turn to Christ.'

The great day came a year later when Mr. Staniford made the 1,000 miles journey to see them.
Many erroneous ideas were put right and many a
laugh enjoyed over early mistakes. With the knowledge already gained they were able to decide on the
policy of opening work first among the pagans, who
are rapidly being absorbed into Islam. Journeys
were taken in the district, French officials, interviewed, gave encouragement, and finally a first
centre selected, Kounkane, among the Foulacounda
tribe, 'just in the transitional belt : in the north
are staunch Moslems, just south of us totally pagan.'

The next year was mainly spent in building.
Labour was difficult to obtain, so an unusual amount
was done by the two Crusaders themselves, felling
timber, hauling and sawing it up. ' Physically we
became tired as we put in the concrete foundations,
laid some 8,000 sun-baked bricks each weighing
nearly 20 lbs., and fitted rafters each of which took
three men an hour to fix. How wonderfully the
Lord kept us rejoicing in spite of the terrific heat,
with the thought of speaking of Him to these people
who had never heard and in many cases never seen
a white man. After our evening meal we would go
off into the village to tell the people of Jesus and His
salvation. Tiredness was soon forgotten in the joy of
sitting in the midst of a crowd of dark-brown men,

women and kiddies, preaching the Word to them.
Night after night the interest was maintained as the
folk crowded round. "We don't want Mohamme-
danism," was the statement of the chief who soon
after gave his heart to the Lord and began at once
telling others of the peace he had through Jesus.
After a while others, too, gave their hearts to the
Lord.'

Actually the first clear-cut case of conversion was
a Moslem lad named Ooma So. He had been with
them for some time and then, one day when out on
trek, Ted Gibbons wrote, ' I sat on my bed and
Ooma on his and had a talk to him about the Lord.
He knows the persecution he will get and that he will
be hated by his family but he said that he wanted
to follow Jesus. So he came over to my bed and
there we knelt down and he prayed aloud for the
first time to the Lord Jesus.'

Eighteen months later we hear, ' Ooma has gone
through much, for his father is a noted Moslem. He
was kept out of his home for three months. His
father vowed he would poison him. Persecution
spread through the village. But through it all he
has stood firm and to-day is rejoicing in salvation.
God has graciously spoken to him from time to time
in dreams, confirming his faith. The people all
know him for a follower of Jesus. He is the only
light in that dark Moslem village, and his last words
to us were, " Pray for me." '

The dead hand of Islam lies on that land.
' Already since we came out here we have been dis-

mayed to see people accepting Islam, and mosques being built in various places.' Now a greater than Mohammed, One who was manifested to destroy the works of the Devil, has arrived on the scene. The little band of three will grow. Senegal, Portuguese Guinea (to which the first four Crusaders have just gone), the 50,000 pagans of Northern French Guinea, all shall hear, though it may take fifty Crusaders to do it.

CHAPTER XI

THE WAY UP IS DOWN

IT is a good thing that God said, ' I will build again the tabernacle . . . which is fallen down,' and added, ' the glory of this latter house shall be greater than of the former.' For who of us would have any hope unless the Lord picked up the bits of the crashes we make and re-made our lives better than ever ? Wonderful God !

Some years back a small mission was founded to evangelize Liberia. A party of workers set out in high hopes. They loved the Lord. They loved the people. The land lay open before them, for Liberia is the only remaining African republic, its president and government being purely negro, and it welcomes missionaries.

It takes more than zeal, however, to run a mission smoothly. The missionaries must know how to love one another. In this case, as is the shattering experience of many Christian organizations, there was failure in this respect. Some had to leave the field through ill-health, some remained on, but things were not running smoothly.

The Holy Spirit was also speaking to Horace and Carol Davey on another matter. They were stationed near the coast and the word kept coming to them, ' Lift up your eyes. What about the countless multitudes further inland ? ' The call became

plainer and plainer. They must inaugurate a forward movement. Yet how could they? It was the
time of the world's financial crisis. It was most
unlikely that the home council would agree. There
was not even harmony on the field. No, they could
not go forward yet.

To a man of God the cost of disobedience to
the Holy Spirit is far greater than the cost of obedience. Disaster followed disaster : a fire on the
station : a severe illness : the birth of a baby girl
with a deformed foot. There seemed nothing left
to do but to leave their work on the coast, not to
speak of the interior, and return to a church in
Canada, their homeland.

They went, swelling the number who had come
home to five, leaving only three on the field. At
this point the home council stepped in. The work
had involved a great deal of expense. It was
decided to close it down. But, thank God, scratch a
true missionary by attempting to shut down the work
and, though meek and mild on the surface, you find
a lion beneath ! With one voice those back at home
and those on the field cried, ' Though we starve, this
shall not be. If the mission is closed down, we
will still go on.' It had taken the rod of adversity to
sting the Daveys into the action which they would
not take beneath the quiet beams of prosperity.
How truly is disaster God's blessing in disguise.
Where would Moses or Joseph or Job or a hundred
others have been but for their dark valleys ?

Horace and Carol Davey, Edward and Winifred

Hancox, and Percy Clubine, all back in Canada, combined to find God's way for a forward movement in Liberia : not just a re-occupation of existing centres, but the fulfilment of the vision given to the Daveys, the Gospel to every tribe still unreached.

At this crucial moment they met the Crusade in Canada. To their surprise and joy they learned that only a few months previously we had been led to publish Inland Liberia as a future field. Here was God's answer. More than that, here was God's way of bringing the vision to fulfilment. For as they learned how God had led the Crusade these years, they had their eyes opened in a new way to the secrets of faith. The first step the Daveys took was to claim and receive as a seal the healing of the little girl's foot by the treatment of a specialist. Then Horace Davey wrote to Alfred Ruscoe : ' Four years ago on the field we were led definitely to step out in faith for this field, but the fear of man was too much for us and we withheld and have ever since been condemned. Now I wonder if you will consider us as fellow-labourers in the Crusade? We are not asking you for anything but your prayers and co-operation. We believe that not only will we ourselves go back, but that five others will return with us.'

They refused to accept funds from the Crusade, though having none of their own, and have persisted in this attitude of independent faith. Not that such a position is necessary or normal, but it may be that, after having turned back on the previous occasion, God has especially led them this way that they might prove Him for themselves. In January, 1938, they set out once more for the field. With them, according to their faith, were four Crusaders and two independent missionaries. Percy Clubine, their co-worker in Liberia, returned with them. The others were new recruits. The two who had previously returned home, Edward and Winifred Hancox, also joined the Crusade to stand behind them at the home base and became the first members of the Canadian staff. 'At the coast (wrote Horace Davey) we had good contact with the officials and received a royal welcome back. When the natives of the Bassa tribe heard that we were leaving to go inland to the Mano tribe they sent us a typewritten petition, signed by seventy of the local chiefs and townmasters, begging us to return and give them the Word of God. We were waiting on God for special guidance as to where to locate and how to divide the party, so this caused us to reconsider the whole situation. Finally we all got clear guidance, that the brothers Finlay and Carson (independent workers) should advance to the Mano tribe, Percy Clubine and Cyril Holloway to the Gios, and we four trek up country, but remaining in the Bassa tribe, to seek a suitable centre.'

There was no delay in getting to business, as each party had a leader who had previous experience of

LIBERIA

work in Africa. Last farewells were said and the three parties did not meet together again until they held a united conference ten months later. The government gave the utmost help and all three parties were soon established in their tribes. Percy Clubine writes from the Gios, the most inland of the three, ' We have a fine opportunity here. Figures are only rough as yet, but there are five clan chiefs, two paramount chiefs and a population of about 50,000. The largest town has 600 huts. The people are a fine type, but the least civilized of any that I have seen yet. The women especially seem to have no sense of ordinary propriety. We have made a start at the language, but it is quite a puzzle as yet. We have a preaching service, and medical work is just roaring along. Last Monday we must have turned away seventy people for lack of medicines.'

Later he wrote, ' We have made three treks and visited the town of every chief. Everywhere we met with a great welcome from the people who almost without exception have never heard the name of Jesus. In nearly every case they asked us how to pray. I have a great burden for these souls and pray continually that the Holy Spirit will do a mighty work in their hearts.' ' The countryside here on the whole is beautiful (adds Cyril Holloway). At times we would scale rocky slopes covered with pine-apples. The rice has just started to grow, making spots look like a rich green carpet amid the woods. Many profess to accept Jesus, so we are trusting God to make such work the nucleus of the indigenous church.[1]

The Daveys and the independent workers have had a similar experience. The Crusader staff now numbers eight. In addition, the three remaining members of the original mission stayed on the field and joined another society instead of returning to Canada. Thus out of what appeared to be a misfortune has arisen a work twice as large. In place of eight, there is now a combined staff of fifteen working in brotherly harmony in four centres and with an objective of a further ten workers to complete the task. If God finds faith on the earth, though the enemy comes in one way, he surely goes out in ten.

CHAPTER XII

'VERILY THOU SHALT BE FED'

ACCORDING to our usual custom, we gathered together on the evening of the third anniversary of Mr. Studd's death, July 16, 1934. We were talking over what God had done through him and since, in sending the ten, fifteen and twenty-five, when a man, known only to one of us, walked into our midst. He had come on quite another errand. He had travelled 50 miles to find the secret of the Spirit-filled life. He had been in contact with one of our number some months previously, and although nothing had been said on the subject the fellowship had awakened in him a longing for a deeper experience of Christ. He remained three days with us. As is our usual method, we did not lightly encourage him to go all the way with God. We showed him from the Scriptures that the Holy Spirit, Whose full indwelling he desired to realize, changed the nature of those whom He possessed from living for themselves to living for others. Through us He travails. By means of us He finds the time and money and lives necessary for the spread of the Gospel. Through us He often answers both our own prayers and those of others for the men and munitions for God's war. Those who will have the Holy Spirit will have the Sufferer for mankind as well as the Saviour of mankind indwelling them, and will be changed into His likeness. It was for this reason that Christ said to those who sought this way of life, ' Sit down first and count the cost.'

However, this brother was on fire for God's best and declared himself willing to drink of the cup and be baptized with the baptism of the Lord Jesus, abandoning himself by faith to the full control of the Holy Spirit.

During the course of those three days with us he naturally heard at our daily meetings of our next objective. With the completion of the twenty-five we had waited on God to find out what number of new workers we should ask for in the coming year, and the answer had come—fifty. This was double the previous year and considerably more than the whole staff of three years before, and it meant £5,000 to send them out ; but we had come to know the God of miracles by now through so many infallible proofs, that I think we found it easier to trust Him for fifty this year than for ten three years previously. Not that faith can ever be said to be truly easy ; for to the fallen reason it always has the appearance of a blind plunge in the dark, and can only be maintained by persistent adherence in the Spirit to the promises of God, ' enduring as seeing Him who is invisible.'

During the days this brother was with us he enthusiastically added his faith and prayer to ours for the coming of this number, but he was on dangerous ground. There was nothing about him which gave us any inkling that he possessed more than an income sufficient for his present occupation, but we were to learn differently.

He left us. Ten days later we received an ordinary unregistered letter. When opened there was seen to be from this brother a cheque for £6,000, £5,000 for the fifty and the extra £1,000 to be used as the Lord directed ! Apparently, on returning home, he had continued to pray for the fifty. Then the Holy Spirit spoke to him. Was he altogether His ? ' Yes, Lord.' Was all he had His ? ' Yes.' Then he must learn that a man of God must not pray for what he can himself pay. He is always himself the first sufferer, the first giver, as was God Himself. He must always answer his own prayers up to the limit of his ability, then he will have authority with God to receive from Him all else that he cannot himself give. Hence the cheque, and in one gift the full supply. Once more we were ' like them that dream.' Within a fortnight of our asking the Lord for this number so much greater than any in the past, all the finance had been supplied.

There only remained the coming forward of the volunteers, and these arrived in a steady stream till the number was complete. They included, as usual, some who were later rejected, others being accepted in their places, for although we only accept candidates who have been through one of the established training colleges, they all have to come and live at headquarters for a while. By this means we observe whether they are men and women of the Holy Ghost, and they have an opportunity to decide whether they are truly one with the principles of the Crusade. With some it takes time, with others there are further preparations to be made, such as the learning of a continental language; so that it was not till some time later that we had completed the outgoing of these thirty-two men and eighteen women to ten different fields.

Such increases in our numbers brought feeding problems which we had never anticipated. Led out by God, as before explained, to depend on Him personally for household needs we had never reckoned on a family of forty or forty-five; but all these years, without a human being knowing our condition from week to week, we can say to the glory of God that we have never lacked a meal.

Nor has debt been allowed. To ensure this, arrangements were made to pay at the door even for the daily supplies of bread and milk. In earlier years I must admit that the burden weighed heavily on me, although it was not I, but Pauline (and latterly Mrs. Purves) who looked after the catering, so I don't know what they must have felt! I used to alternate between weeks in the sunlight and weeks in the shadows. The Lord did a new thing some years back and by His grace I have learned something of that secret by which the eye and ear are kept closed to Satan's suggestions of doubt and fear and kept in singleness of gaze on God, the place where the word of Jesus Christ becomes true, 'If thine eye is single, thy whole body shall be full of light.'

I remember one early and outstanding deliver-

119

ance, when the household numbered only ten. I was going off for four days of meetings and was leaving Pauline with only 4s. 6d. in the house. We had some prayer before parting and told each other that we should meet again to hear of God's deliverances. All the same, it was a test for us both. When I returned I learned that two hours after I had gone a large hamper arrived at the door from the other end of London. It was taken in and opened before the assembled household, and they had a praise meeting round it. It contained, not special delicacies which could only be an addition to ordinary food, but all the necessities for several meals—leg of mutton, potatoes, bread and cheese, the very things needed, and a box of chocolates ' for the Grubblets from a raven.' Weeks after we learned the history of the hamper. We were at tea, in their Kensington flat, with a brother and sister whom we had met only about twice before. The sister took Pauline aside and said, ' I don't know whether my brother would like me saying this, but I thought I would tell you of a strange guidance he had some weeks back. You remember receiving a hamper ? Well, early that morning, when my brother was having his quiet time, the Lord told him to go out and order it and send it to you. I was wondering whether it met some particular need ? '

Another wonderful provision of the Lord has been a regular supply for the past six years of what now amounts to tons of potatoes, lentils, rice and oatmeal. It was particularly wonderful because the

beginning of the supply came just after we obeyed
God in taking on the feeding of the household. A
few weeks later we entered the only period of extreme
testing that we had, when our only food for a week
was bread and cheese. We were at dinner one day
when a van drove up and deposited half a ton of
potatoes. Next day came two hundredweight sacks
of oatmeal, and a few days later two of lentils. They
were from a Christian gentleman whom I had met
only twice at meetings, and who even yet has never
been to our headquarters ; but through his goodness
we have never since been without lentils and oatmeal, and potatoes in season.

Indeed we are usually able to tell what has been
the crop of the season ! One apple year we received
over a ton within a few weeks, but all were most
acceptable. I think we tasted every form there is
of preparing apples for the table !

Beyond all special instances of deliverance stands
out the fact of the unfailing regularity of supply
all these years. It still remains a wonder to me
when I look back on the many times in which I
have enquired of Pauline how the houshold funds
are, to be told that she is using the last pound ; yet
through all these 2,920 days the barrel of meal has
never failed, the fresh gift has come along just in
time. Sometimes even larger numbers have to be
catered for. At our conferences at the end of each
month we sit down sixty to eighty in number. At
our last conference, from Saturday afternoon to
Monday morning, I asked the candidate in charge of

the kitchen how things had been going, and she replied that there had been only 4*s*. 6*d*. in the morning, but during the day 10 lbs. of cheese, two joints of beef, 5 lbs. of sausages, pots of jam and marmalade, biscuits, swiss rolls, tins of peas, potatoes had arrived, practically all from unknown sources. We can only speak from experience at the home end, but, were the Crusaders on the fields to write of their tests and deliverances also, what book could contain them ?

CHAPTER XIII

WOMEN BLAZE THE TRAIL

' THEY are surging round me. One has caught
      hold of my trousers. I loosen his hand. I look
and see between 300 and 400 Moslems all shouting
and swearing and threatening. Now one man has
jumped up and slaps me hard on my face. I turn
my other cheek, but he does not heed it. I say to
him, " I have no enmity in my heart against you !
Shake hands ! " But no. He is so bigoted that he
won't. Soon I am pushed down and am in the very
middle of the crowd. Immediately from all quarters
I am punched and kicked. . . .' Ron Davis had
gone down into the bazaar to rescue two schoolboys
who had been enticed away to be smuggled to some
remote spot. The cry had gone up, ' He is kid-
napping Mohammedan boys,' and the crowd rushed
in blind rage on him. ' All over a couple of
schoolboys ? (writes Ron). No ! They are souls for
whom Christ died ! As Christ laid down His life
for me, I am prepared to lay mine down for the
brethren if needs be.'

Indeed he might have done, for this was Haripur,
chief town in the Hazara district of the North-West
Frontier Provinces of India, that troublesome region
where it is estimated that ' one in twenty is a poten-
tial murderer.'

To this field, and the neighbouring country or

Kashmir, God has called the Crusade in recent
years. All honour to Him, who out of weakness
makes us strong, that the first missionaries to settle
among these people were two women, Hilda Ashby
and Cara Robertson.[1] Twenty-five years ago, having left comfortable homes in England, they travelled
up through India to its northern frontiers, until
they reached Haripur. They found it to be the
central town of a 'tahsil' or district including 380
villages.

The town itself contained the usual ' motley crowd
of Hindu shopkeepers, fat and richly dressed ; tall,
sinewy Mohammedans ; peasants from the hills ;
religious mendicants ; frowsy and lousy beggars ;
cheeky modern schoolboys ; and veiled females.'
Out in the villages they met the real natives of
the Hazara, ' tall and well-built, with oval faces, fair
skins and fine, well-marked features. The usual
thing for a young man is to adorn himself with little
curls, and, with a rose stuck in his puggree and a
waistcoat embroidered in crimson and magenta silk,
he presents a most jaunty appearance. He has
admirable manners, this raw country bumpkin ;
with his hand on his heart he gives a deep bow as he
salutes one. The villagers of the older generation
look very dignified in their long, immensely wide
trousers. Young, unmarried girls are often exceed-
ingly pretty. The men are very good horsemen and
good at sports. Passionate, unpractical and alto-

[1] Cara Robertson was called to higher service in May, 1939,
aged sixty-two.

124

gether unreliable, they are notwithstanding attractive, full of fun and responsive.'

The first home of the women was just a native mandi, where the camel caravans 'load for the long journeys to the Back o' Beyond.' Their next move was to get a permanent footing in the country by buying ' a small piece of land on which wheat was growing ' and living in tents at one end of it. In this small beginning lay the germ of the future lines on which the work was to develop. Before they reaped their first tiny harvest of wheat a Moslem young woman made an open confession of Christ. ' She was at once turned out of her home, so there was nothing else to do but take her in as our sister. Then came our wheat harvest. It was a memorable occasion when Cara Robertson went out to cut it with a pair of scissors ! It filled a large tin box. But we had begun to understand the " pattern shown us on the Mount." We had come to a Mohammedan country. There would be a crying need for a place where boycotted and persecuted Christians can start their lives afresh on Christian principles. Here was our first young convert. Here was land for her to work on ; and here was also a trunk of wheat to keep her in food ! " Why, it's a farm ! " I exclaimed. " It's a Mission Farm we've got."

' Year by year, as with joy and gladness we now gather in the golden grain on our sixteen acre property, our memories go back to that first harvest and we see what great things the Lord has done for us.

' After that first girl there was a continual stream

of converts, but so wonderful was the ordering from above that we never had more at one time than we could manage—five. If one went away, another would be sure to come. But when they went to their homes we knew they could not stay long if they remained true to Christ. Invariably they would return, often with a sad story of persecution or escape by the skin of their teeth from those who sought their lives. Yet, through these visits, the Gospel spread to villages inaccessible to us, and seldom did a convert go home without influencing one or other of his relatives.'

To the wheat growing was added a grape fruit plantation, crops of clover and cotton, and a weaving industry. One year they had several visitations of locusts, ' just as a big field of cucumbers was sprouting and a field of cotton showing green. A small gathering of Christians was in the prayer room when the head-gardener, a Mohammedan, came to the door and said, " The locusts are coming. Pray that they may be sent away." A little while afterwards one of the men called me to see " a wonderful thing." He took me through the orchard and into the flower garden, where not a locust was to be seen, but just the other side of the wall he showed me the Mohammedan graveyard, where every little bush and tree was red with the locusts resting after their flight. " I have never seen anything so extra-ordinary," said the young Mohammedan. " Truly your God does answer prayer ! " '

Through the years ' the mission community has

grown to many hundreds,' but never has there been such a wave of inquiry as at present, and with corresponding opposition. 'It is a wonderful time we are living in (writes Miss Ashby). We have never experienced it like this before, but the opposition is getting fiercer and fiercer. The people are coming in numbers to inquire about Christianity, and we appear again and again in the native newspapers. The public are warned against us as "thieves of religion." "Wake up, O Moslems !" they write, "your religion is in danger." The greater part of the population is for us, but there is a very bitter section of Mohammedans against us. They stir the children to call out after the Christians, and the roughs to set on them and beat them. Every Friday they lecture against us in the mosque. It is proclaimed a sin to enter the mission compound. The goldsmiths came to a service. On leaving they were waylaid in the bazaar, dragged by the mob into the mosque and badly beaten. One man is being badly ostracized. His wife won't feed him. But he is town crier and yesterday stood on the bridge, where the traffic is heaviest, and sang for all he was worth, "Sound the chorus loud and clear, He has brought salvation near, None so precious, none so dear, Jesus Christ our Saviour." It needs great courage to be openly a Christian in this dark Mohammedan city.'

For the three months of intense heat each year the women moved across the frontier into the glorious mountains and valleys of Kashmir, the Switzerland of India. ' We feel refreshed as we lift our eyes away from the gross darkness of these Central Asian villages to the pure snow-capped peaks untouched by the foot of man. We see the snow summits of the mighty Harmook reflected in the lake from the front of our houseboat. The early morning sun rising behind creates dazzling beauty, while the view is especially lovely at sunset, when the sun sinks behind the mountains and the water becomes the colour of old silver and rich gold.'

Ultimately they turned this summer camp into a second Mission farm, at Sopor on the lovely Wular lake, thus setting permanent foot in Kashmir. They found the people much akin to the Hazara folk. ' One must always remember that they both are artist nations. The Kashmiris are a people of con-trasts—excessive kindness and refined cruelty, revelling in beauty and countenancing indescribable dirt ! One picks one's way through the foulest alleys with one's umbrella up, lest one should receive a shower of dirty water from an upper window on one's head. Yet as one glances at the windows one notices in each a separate design in wood carving. Sitting just above a drain, from which arises an unspeakable stench, is a tailor embroidering, blending soft colours together in an exquisite design, which has been copied from the mountains and waters, rice fields and flowers, of his country. His artistic soul does not like the filth, but he is too indolent to remedy it. So he looks the other way ! '

The years have taken toll of the old warriors. Their whole hearts and lives have been absorbed in their ministry to the people. Miss Ashby has taken no furlough these twenty-five years, and Miss Robertson only once for six months. They were joined in 1926 by Miss Ruth Ashby, ' who had come for a visit which has now been extended fourteen years ! '

The need of the millions of Kashmir, coupled with the future security of their own work, sent them back to God in urgent prayer for reinforcements. His answer was to lead them in 1933 into association with the Crusade, forming the Kashmir and Frontier Mission of the W.E.C. Five new workers have already joined them, new centres have been opened at Baramulla and Muzufferabad, and a more recent development has been the establish-ment of twelve village schools where 500 Moslem boys receive daily Bible instruction.

The biggest leap forward of all has been a 200-mile stride by Arthur and Mary Downing into southern Kashmir, over the rugged Banihal Pass, where ' the mountains rose up like a wall in front of us (wrote Miss Ashby), and we found ourselves gradually ascending. After some 6 miles I began to feel I would be glad when I reached the top, and asked how much further on it was. " Oh, about 12 more miles ! " the driver told me. I held my breath as we zigzagged up the perpendicular wall, with glorious views behind and the valley spread beneath, looking so peaceful with its little scattered homesteads, and the wild precipitous mountains rising up behind. It seemed unbelievable that any lorry could climb such heights. It was an intense relief when we at last passed into a small tunnel at the summit of the pass. . . .' A day later, far down on the other side of the range, they came to 'a pine-clad hill, on the higher slopes of which lies the village of Batote.'

It was here that the Downings settled, at the junction of roads leading to the three districts of Bhadarwah, Kishtawah, and Udhampur, where there is no other missionary witness among 370,000 people. Beyond these again lie the three provinces of Punch, Mirpur and Riasi, with an unreached population of 900,000. Within a few months they wrote, ' It has been just wonderful how God has brought leading men to our doorstep and prompted them to bid us enter their districts. Hearty invitations have been extended to us to go into Bhardawah, Kishtawah and Mirpur. I wish I could impress on you what open doors these are.' Again, ' The Lord is bringing all sorts of people right to us for miles, and prejudice is being broken down. A Government road official visited us. He wanted to talk of wisdom ! He came and heard of the wisdom of God and the new birth. Then he told how he had picked up a muddy piece of paper. It was '' The Way of Salvation,'' and as he read what he could he said, '' This is good.'' He asked his clerk where such a thing could have come from and received the answer, " Oh, a padre sahib has come near Batote to convert the people." Although we have in stock only such very simple medicines as we know how to use, yet in eight months we have had some 2,000 patients.' The door lies wide open. A Moslem country actually inviting Christian missionaries to enter ! We are thankful to God for such an opportunity, and say with Caleb of old, ' Let us go up at once and possess it.'

CHAPTER XIV

COURAGE, NOT SAFETY

A FRAIL looking, quiet woman was on board a liner travelling to India. She had said good-bye to parents and sisters in a lovely, old-world home not far from the King's private residence in Windsor Great Park. Her father was one of England's leading metallurgists. She was a doctor. For some years she had ministered to the bodies and souls of India's masses in a mission hospital, but the call of the regions beyond had been constantly sounding in her ears. There in the north lay the land of Nepal. Enclosed in its mountain fastnesses were 6,000,000 people who, through the intense conservatism of its rulers, were still shut out from all 'Western influences.' For 500 miles its frontier marched with India's. Crowds of villages swarmed along its length, where the great plains roll over the border to the depth of a few miles, until they are halted by the mighty wall of the Himalayas. Thus 3,000,000 of the population are 'plainsmen,' Indian by race and language, though Nepalese subjects, and 3,000,000 'hill men.'

On her return to England, in her quiet home away from the rush of hospital life, she had time to listen to God. The voice was unmistakable. She was to pull up stakes and move on. Others could do the hospital work. But on the 500-mile frontier

132

she had learned that for the western 250 miles there was no missionary witness. The people move to and fro over five great passes into inland Nepal, without a person to tell them that the Father's arms lie open to them.

She was frail, and a single woman. Her daring project was to go and live in one of these frontier villages. It meant that no white companion would be near her and no human protection in case of illness and danger. No wonder that the committee of her mission, keen though they were for India's evangelization, did not feel that they could take responsibility for such a venture. She could go, if she was sure of her guidance, and their sympathies would be with her, but financially and in every way it must be her own decision. But she was sure of her call.

Surrounded by the comforts and friends of the homeland, perhaps the stark realities of the undertaking did not come home to her. But when the last cable that bound her to loved ones and Christian supporters had been cut, as the liner ploughed its way across the Indian Ocean, in Catherine Harbord's cabin the age-old drama of the brook Jabbok was re-enacted. Fear almost overwhelmed her. 'There wrestled a man with her till the breaking of the day.' 'A great temptation came to me to be allowed to ask to stay in hospital work. The difficulties and possible dangers seemed overwhelming.

133

The Lord made me face it all out in every detail. He told me He had never promised us safety in His service : there was no promise of being kept from sickness, death or worse. But He has promised to save us by bringing us victorious through them. He showed me all that might happen and brought me through till I could say, " Whatever happens, the very worst I can think of, still I can never doubt Him. I shall know that it is part of His loving plan for me." ' Broken, blessed, there rose from her knees in that cabin a new woman, a prince with God who could testify, ' From the moment that I could honestly say this with no reservations, joy and peace flooded my spirit, and He has never let me know fear since.'

She went to Nautanwa, the railhead to one of the five passes, and only found when she was settled there that she had been led to the most important place on the whole of the 500-mile frontier, the only centre where there is a settlement of Nepalese on the Indian side.

She rented and occupied a native Indian house so as to be more one with the people, and for the next eight years lived there alone (except for a few short periods when she was sent elsewhere by her mission), carrying on her ministry of love to bodies and souls. At home the *World Dominion Press* took special note of her work, publishing an article to draw attention to her method of living in an Indian village as perhaps the ideal means of reaching the people. Among the people themselves, as was to be expected after her conflict and victory in the heavenlies, she found herself surrounded, not by dangers, but by gratefulness and love. Her fame spread through all the region, and on several occasions she had the unique privilege of being called by those in authority into the closed land itself. It is wiser not to put in print the details of those thrilling journeys.

'This little native house of Dr. Harbord's', wrote Dr. Morris later, 'is in an excellent position as a dispensary. The square, flanked by native houses of the hillmen's quarter, is used as a threshing floor at this season. The patient bullocks treading out the golden corn, the black coatees and scarlet skirts of the neat little Gurkha women, and the sturdy little hillmen with cheery faces, form a contrast to the Indian quarter, with its rather unkempt women clad in dusky white saris and the sleek servile-looking men with their black tufts of hair. The enormous weekly bazaar, when crowds up to fifteen thousand assemble, is a wonderful opening for the Gospel.' Of this Dr. Harbord herself writes, 'By mid-day it is one mass of people, and it requires patience to get through the crowd at all. Armed with a few Gospels for sale and some hundreds of tracts for free distribution, we push our way here and there. The tracts are eagerly taken. Greetings come from every side. "My son is sick. Give me some medicine." "Don't you remember me, you cured me three years ago?" Many are from over the Nepal border. They have come from some of the four thousand villages of

135

these districts. Ask them of their religion. The answer is Hindu or Mohammedan. There may be a few Buddhists. Christians? Not one. Many are bitterly opposed to Christ. Many are indifferent. Many are hopeless. Active powers of evil are felt everywhere, manifested in word or glance, in the signs of idol worship, in the callousness shown to the sick and poor. Moving among them, knowing that the Lord died for these very people and that not one seems to know or care, is almost more than one can bear. And yet, just because He has died for them, He gives us faith to believe that He is calling out from among them a people for Himself. The bazaar often re-echoes to the shouts of " Victory to Gandhi," but we know the victory is to the Lord Most High.'

Her vision reached far beyond the occupation of one railhead on the frontier. What of the four others? What of the fact that no single reinforcement had joined her these eight years? ' Pray ye the Lord of the harvest that He will send forth labourers into His harvest.' This Catherine Harbord did for many a day and night through those lonely years. ' Why art Thou silent, O my God ? ' ' How long, O Lord ? ' must often have been her cry. Yet it was the old, old story. Life was to come out of death. Physical weakness began to trouble her. All was not well. An operation, which could only be safely performed in England, was necessary without delay. Had God forgotten those needy multitudes? Was He deaf to her cry? It looked like it, for she well knew that she might never return herself, so that, instead of sending reinforcements, God seemed to be allowing His only representative to be removed. Yet does not all Scripture teach us that man has to go to his extremity to give God His opportunity?

Dr. Harbord had heard of the W.E.C. and its field in Kashmir. She knew of its calling—to every unevangelized area. Then why not the Nepal Border? She wrote to the field leader asking if there was one, specially if possible a doctor, who could take her place, if only for a year, and save the work from closing down. There was. Dr. Wilfred Morris had been spending time gaining medical experience under Sir Henry Holland at Quetta. We had already been in correspondence with him about opening a possible field on the Nepal Border when the S.O.S. from Dr. Harbord reached him. The connection was so obvious that he had no doubt about this being the next stage in God's plan, and he had crossed India and arrived at Nautanwa before we heard the first word about it in London! In fact, Dr. Harbord herself arrived to inform us! Having already noted with much approval the lines of her work as described in *World Dominion*, we were equally sure that this co-operation was not merely the filling of a temporary gap, but the answer to her prayer of years.

The operation was successful, and at the same time a re-arrangement in the policy of her mission left her free to suggest her return as a member of a Nepal Border Mission of the W.E.C. The apparent

137

end of her hopes and labours had turned out to be God's way of changing a one-man work into a mission to occupy the whole 250 miles of country. God does not suffer His faithfulness to fail. Dr. Harbord is now back on her beloved frontier with three co-workers, besides two independent missionaries at Nautanwa, one a woman doctor. She reckons that another five workers are necessary to man the trade routes, by which time she has faith that the barriers will break down and the closed land open.

Meanwhile an occasional lifting of the veil shows how deeply the ministry of love is penetrating the hearts of many who have not yet made an open confession of Christ. News of our reinforcements were sent to the headquarters of an Indian anti-Christian organization—the Gospel's bitterest opponent. They announced the personal visit of a well-known leader to Nautanwa to boycott the missionaries. Busy preparations were made with banners and open-air meetings. A volley of shots announced his arrival. ' We heard that there were two thousand people listening to him. His opening remarks were the same old lies and accusations, that we had only come here to spoil their women and girls. After half an hour the two thousand had diminished to sixty. One or two courageous ones asked questions : " If these men are giving us light and we are in darkness, why should we not listen to them ? " " These men love us and treat our sick. Why should we leave them when they love us ? " " If we leave them and come to you, will you send doctors and men to love us and care for our sick ? " The only reply from the great man was, " You fools, to listen to their lies," and with this the meeting broke up. The next night they had another attempt to boycott us, but this was not a success, for the Outcastes, Nepalese and Mohammedans made a pact to keep away from their meeting place. I tell you it was great.'

CHAPTER XV

A CLAMANT CALL

MEANWHILE a further call from India stirred us to prayer and consecration, as it did all the church of Christ. News reached us of the declarations of the Depressed Class leader, Dr. Ambedkar, publicly renouncing Hinduism for himself and the 70,000,000 of his people, who groaned beneath the tyranny of its caste system, and of his call to them to seek another religion which could offer equality of opportunity and privilege. We were thrilled to hear the reports from many centres of the crowds pressing into the Kingdom. Above all, we rejoiced at the results of the sane and thorough investigation into the value of the Outcaste Mass Movements, which had been undertaken by Dr. Pickett and the other members of the Commission appointed to the task by the National Christian Council in India, a survey which, published under the title of ' Christian Mass Movements in India,' abundantly vindicated the reality of the work of the Spirit among them. We knew that in this greatest call to the church of our generation we must take our share, and one morning, after half a day of prayer at our London headquarters, we unitedly dedicated ourselves to start a mission to the Outcastes.

We made inquiries from experts, including Dr.

Pickett himself, concerning the areas where we should find the largest number of Outcastes without a missionary witness, and all pointed us to the United Provinces, especially to a district called Basti. What was our surprise when reference to a map revealed that this was the very district in which Nautanwa is located, and that the U.P. has as its northern frontier the very 250 miles of the Nepal Border for which we had accepted responsibility! The guidance was obvious. We could carry on a combined Outcaste-Nepali work. We wrote in this strain to Dr. Morris, only to receive perfect confirmation in a letter from him, which crossed ours, saying that a neighbouring missionary had suggested the very same district. So the matter was settled.

The first centre, 'where there are 1,000,000 people and no Christian,' was not found easily. In 1936 Wilfred Morris 'commenced to seek out a place, but the Ark of the Lord did not rest.' In 1937 ' definite guidance came that Domariaganj was to be our first station. When we visited it, our hearts were filled with a deep prayerful assurance that there the work should start. Villages are everywhere, as if they were pepper sprinkled from a castor. We had in view this large village with a country court to which many come for litigation. On arrival we found the villagers all very friendly, partly due to the first man we met, who had been to Nautanwa and knew of our dispensary there! So God had

141

prepared the way for us. Across the river a huge
market was in progress. The Government assistant
doctor is most desirous for me to come, and helped
us in negotiating for one of the Indian houses that
seemed most suitable.'

'The Indians are quite at home and undismayed
by any magnificence when they come,' wrote Nancy
Morris later. 'The house is on the courtyard plan,
so popular here, and we have a fine wide verandah
which we use a good deal, eating and sleeping there.
If any doctor saw Wilf's dispensary, with all its
home-made gadgets and lack of white tiles—well,
well—I tell him he might get struck off the medical
roll ! However, the Lord blesses the medicine and
provides for it in a wonderful way.'

The fame of Dr. Morris' wizardry with the knife
soon spread.

'Our courtyard to-day is a great centre of attraction, for it is rumoured that the white doctor is going
to " cut about " or operate. Has not the mother of
Raji—groping in darkness as all the village knows—
received new hope of sight before the coming
" Feringi " ? Did he not shine a mysterious light
into her eyes and then say words of comfort and
hope ? After which he prayed in the name of one
Jesus. But see, here comes the white one—and the
crowd hushes for a moment. But not for long ! No
sooner have the sahib and memsahib gone in with
the headman and patient than the crowd makes a
determined rush at the door, and forty or so are in
before the doctor sees that something must be done !

Firm remonstration avails for a brief space and the door is barred again. Two packing cases and a plank across form the crude but effective operation table; the old woman is helped up, laid on a mackintosh sheet, and the doctor drops a few drops into her eyes and turns to superintend instrument sterilization. In a breathing space he turns to the watchers and explains that he has only power by trusting in His Saviour whom they know not. And the crowd are astonished to see the doctor close his eyes, fold his hands and begin to pray for healing and wisdom and forgiveness of sins for all. Excitement reaches a high pitch as the operation opens; with difficulty the headman prevents spectators from thronging too near, and the comments form a steady buzz.

'Suddenly there is a greater disturbance. The whole door gives way and some twenty more people enter noisily. The cataract, a pearl-like globe, is just coming out and is given to a relative who shows it round the ring. A low murmur of astonishment follows. The bandage is applied and the doctor heaves a sigh of relief, for only he knows how much prayer accomplished under such awful conditions.

' "Yes," says the headman, "without doubt Jesus' name is the mighty power that enables these miracles to be done. Thank God He has sent you to help the poor." '

Out in the villages they used the same combination of practical love and spiritual teaching. An anxious husband comes in one evening. 'Is that you,

Mahabir ? ' Morris asked. ' There is a stir in the shadow of the verandah and the lantern's dim light reveals a man. " Yes, sir, I have come again, for my wife is in pain." Soon we were walking down the dimly-lit bazaar road, with its inches deep of dust, on our way to the Outcastes' homes. As we entered the neatly kept, though small courtyard, the lantern revealed the low string cot with mother and infant lying in it. When I had bound up the wound, the husband produced some English soap with great to-do, and poured water over my hands as I washed. " Your wrist is still dirty, doctor ! " he exclaimed. I saw he alluded to a black stain left by some strong caustic medicine. " Why, brother, that won't come off with soap and water. You see, it's in the skin." " Do you know," I went on, " there's another stain that won't come off, however much you wash it with soap and water. It's the stain of sin left on the heart of every man, on mine, on yours. But there is a way to cleanse that stain, for the blood of Jesus Christ, God's Son, cleanseth us from all sin." Shadows fell across the listening figures of man and wife as the wind stirred the lantern flames. Oh, that this first hearing of the way of salvation may bring forth fruit in this Outcaste home.'

The first signs came a year later. Nancy Morris wrote, ' A week ago the husband of the Chamar (Outcaste) woman, who works for us, came and said that his people wanted Wilf to go and tell them " what they had to do." We had a pretty good idea that their eyes were on loaves and fishes and we

THE FIVE FIELD LEADERS

(1) S. J. Staniford, West Africa.   (2) A. P. Symes, Colombia.
(3) J. Harrison, Belgian Congo.
(4) A. Thorne, Spanish Guinea.   (5) W. M. Morris, India.

all decided that we could not offer any worldly bait
to persuade them to become Christians.

'A large number gathered. Can you see it? A
little clearing between their mud and thatch houses.
The circle of men, lean, dark, pulling their dirty
sheets around them as they squatted in front of us,
the lantern light revealing the women standing
behind, holding their babies. They had put a string
bed for us to sit on, but as usual Wilf preferred to
squat down with them. Very clearly he put to them
the Gospel and its eternal gain, but also made it plain
that we could not help them in a material way more
than we had done.

'We left them to think it over, praying that
spiritual desire might be born in their hearts. Yesterday the same man came again and said they would
all become Christians if we would settle them down
in a little village, so that people could say, " These
are the Sahib's people." The proposition was not
without attraction. How nice to have a Christian
village. We could give regular teaching and get
them converted and to become evangelists. Pleasant
enough thoughts ; but in reality it would be taking
a handful of heathens from one place to another,
while they would sink into contentment, saying,
" Are we not the Sahib's caste ? " As we spread it
before the Lord, we both knew that to do this would
be to build in wood, hay and stubble.'

Then ten days later : ' We were much encouraged
this evening when we went down to the Chamar
group, by their willingness to take the first step to

becoming Christians (in spite of the fact that their hopes *re* a new village were dashed) by setting aside a little piece of ground for worship. If they do this it will be a definite sign of their intention to become Christians and receive instruction.'

The battle still rages. The bitterly anti-Christian sect now so active in India got to work. ' The piece of worship ground was prepared and we taught them to pray, but these people warned them against us and our doctrine. They were frightened, and apparently all desire to learn more of Christ has gone. *But* Jesus is still far above all.'

The work is in its embryo stage and there will be a different story to tell in a few years time. Even so, with a staff now of ten, three of whom are still learning the language, Mrs. Morris writes, ' Can you think what a joy it has been to see the work spreading out ? Rudhauli occupied to the east, Baotia Bazaar to the west and Barhni up north on the border.' The hosts of God are marching on.

CHAPTER XVI

WORLD'S STURDIEST MEN

'I HAVE passed through almost tropically hot river valleys,' wrote Wilfred Morris, 'with jungle of bamboo cane and plantains. I forded a river up to my waist when I thought I was gone twice, and stood shivering looking out over the vale as the dying sun tinted the five snowy peaks of Panchula, and handed Tibetan tracts to wizened old Bhotiya herdsmen as they smoked their pipes after the midday meal halt on the mountain side. I reckon I shall have marched 260 miles in twenty days' walking, so shall be glad to get back to the plains. Three days were through the famous Nepalese terai jungle. It was very warm work and an interesting experience ; as at one place, where a colony of monkeys were sunning themselves on a nice strand of sand by the river. It looked very like Pa, Ma and the kids at the seaside ! On one occasion I had an exciting time, as I arrived about 11 p.m., having marched through forest and hilly country where panthers are quite frequently met, and not a hut for miles. The first hut occupant I met came out with a torch thinking I was a ghost ! He was astounded to see me and asked whether I wasn't afraid of animals. On my replying, " My God will help and protect me," he laughed and said, " What gods are any use ? What will you do if a leopard comes at you ? " I replied, " You don't know my God. He is well able to protect and He walks with me." I certainly was cast on the Lord, especially once when something crashed away on the side of the path ! But it was a blessed time, as I prayed along the way.'

The reason for this long trek of Dr. Morris' among scenes very different from Basti was to solve the one remaining major problem that faced the Nepali and Outcaste work. Life on the plains in Indian villages would be intolerable in the hot months. Why not, then, combine a hill and plain work ? The tired workers could move up a few days' journey into the glorious surroundings of the Himalayan foothills and find not only refreshment of body, but ample opportunities for work among the hillmen. So this exploratory trek was undertaken until he came to the place which seemed ideal for the purpose, Lohaghat in the Kumaon Hills. ' Looking from a point about 7,000 feet up one can see a long valley broadening out to two large hills. At the bottom of the right mount is a great area of deodar (cedar) trees, and nestling amongst these is the village of Lohaghat. The view all round is just glorious, and the great rolling hills, with their terraced cultivation and deodar woods, seem completely to enclose us, except for one view where we can see a part of the 150-mile range of eternal snows. These vast giants, only 60 miles away, separate us from Tibet.' ' This place seems an excellent station to which the missionaries from the plains can come in summer. We can work the country around with its many untouched and well-populated valleys.'

Two summers have now been spent there and the opportunities proved plentiful. Even visits to villages are adventurous. ' Crossing the first rise, through a deodar forest, we slithered down a very deep ditch. The first river could only be crossed by leaping from rock to rock. The climb on the other side developed into a crawl, as we levered ourselves up by trees and bushes. Rents in shirt and skin became obvious, the latter before the former ! By this time we had reached a height which gave a grand view of all the surrounding hills. Nestling amongst trees and bushes the next village came into sight. On our playing a few bhajans, out came the folks. Yes, they were very happy to see us, and had spread mats and rugs for us in a shady place. Thus for an hour we had a grand time. . . .'

Occasionally the great religious festivals afford a marvellous opportunity. ' This past week we have been to the Devi Dhura Mela. The 22 miles were knocked off by evening, and we were glad when the summit of the 7,000-foot mountain was reached. Gazing down on this mass of moving humanity, one wondered where any religious significance was found, but the next morning we saw. The crowd moved down the hills headed by dancers, followed by a large buffalo driven unmercifully along. It was the sin sacrifice, the first of hundreds. " Kali wants blood ! " At mid-day the altar gulley was running with blood. After a time of prayer the Crusaders took a stand in the mela. The accordion quickly drew listeners. The crowds just thronged. Our number was supplemented by the arrival of Hindustani Christians. Gospels went like wildfire ; 2,000 tracts changed hands and almost 200 Gospels were sold. We could have disposed of 400.' Summer by summer the work will be continued, although a few permanent hill workers will also be necessary, owing to language difficulties.

Tibet has always been a land of mystery, and no more picturesque figures are to be seen in these mountains and valleys than the sturdy Tibetan and Bhotiya herdsmen. 'The Tibetan drover often passes with his sheep team. They make a striking picture as they drive down their flocks of long-haired, sturdy goats and mountain sheep, each bearing its pack load of borax, wool and salt.' 'One morning, at the mela,' wrote Len Moules, 'a low muttering outside the tent stirred my curiosity. Pulling the tent flap aside I saw a Tibetan Lama twirling his prayer wheel. Next day I heard a drumming on the ground, accompanied by a thick dust that permeated the very canvas. Nearly choking, I hurried outside and saw a whirling ring of tall figures. The drumming increased its speed, as did the dancers. The spinning bodies flung up their girdles as a wheel, till the last effort brought the dance to an exhausted end. The dancers were grotesque, but it was not until one turned full face to me that I gasped audibly —the Tibetan devil dancers. I had heard of them, seen photos taken by privileged men, yet never dreamt I should see them.'

To do any effective work among these, quite a separate region from the Kumaon Hills has had to be entered, right up on the frontier of Tibet—a lonely and rugged region called the Johar Bhot, 60 miles north of Lohaghat, and cut off for five months of the year by the rains, which wash away the only hill track and make the easily-forded mountain streams into impassable rivers. To this hazardous work Len Moules has been called. At first he was alone, and only remained in his mountain fastness during the months that the route was open, but now he has a companion and is praying for several more to man the three still unevangelized valleys leading into Tibet.

The journey from Lohaghat to his station at Munsiari takes six days. ' The approach to Munsiari is a cruel climb, five miles of hand-made stone steps. We left the valley in the evening at about 5,000 feet and attempted this " Jacob's ladder." We finished up in the region of 10,000 feet. Up these stone stairs the Bhotiya sheep and goats, yaks and ponies, all climb and descend. Once in the Munsiari valley we were at the scene of proposed future work. Six or seven villages are inhabited by 7,000 souls. The valley forms a bottleneck at the north which runs as a natural passage to Tibet.

151

'I cannot tell you the feelings of those first few days, 100 miles from the plains, facing the problem of getting meat, eggs, vegetables and milk, none of which had been tasted for five days and no prospect of getting them. So we took it to the Lord in prayer. Two days later, looking down the valley side to the villages that looked so small 2,000 feet below, I saw a man coming up the craggy path, and in his hand a pigeon which he had brought for me. Thus the Lord sent the meat ! Later a small laddie came in with a dish cloth containing eight eggs ; where they had come from I know not, but God had sent the eggs ! Just before dark a man came for medicine, and in *his* dish cloth were some hill green vegetables, so the Lord had not forgotten the veg. ! The dear Lord never leaves anything undone, so I waited for the milk, and after dark a laddie came from the village and with him was a brass vessel of milk.

'Visiting the villages is great fun. Not just a stroll along the promenade ! One village I went to yesterday involved a steep, craggy climb, 300 yards' walk on stones up a stream, straight up the mountain side for about 200 feet, climbing a rocky stairway. I found the village was situated on a series of ridges, and the " main road " was a staircase.

'I have just had to stop this letter as I saw a big head of a goat at my elbow, and on turning round found two men, one holding the goat and another a bowl of rice. They had come with these as gifts in gratefulness for a cataract operation last week-end. They are a jolly, loving crowd, typically Mongolian

and Tibetan. Their hardships and natural difficulties in crossing into Tibet make them supersti-
tious and yet very cheery under every difficulty. The
language is stiff. I have a working knowledge of
Hindi, but this is a corruption of it. They seem to
open their mouths and let the sound pass out. That's
all. After a time I opened my mouth and let the
sound pass out ! They all roared with laughter. But
now I can get on well in making them understand,
though I am afraid I cannot understand them yet.
Still this will come in time. The work is getting a
grip of the people. During the past week about 120
visited me from twenty-five different villages. Each
heard the Gospel message.

' You can understand the joy I had when poring
over a map of the district to see about seventy
villages underlined, which signifies that they have
been represented in the dispensary and have taken
back the Word of God.'

CHAPTER XVII

A ROMANCE IN BRICKS AND MORTAR

ONE morning at our meeting we were discussing the situation at London headquarters. We had again outgrown our housing capacity. What with staff, candidates and guests, we were packing about forty-five into our three houses. Our largest room could only just hold us for the daily meetings and we had to divide into two parties for meals. Leslie Sutton, being in charge of the practical side of things, had been insistent for some months that we ought to enlarge our accommodation, either by acquiring another house or by building, somehow, a hostel to our own specification.

Now we have a well-understood principle among us, about which we often have a little harmless fun, but which is also held and practised in all seriousness. If any one has a conviction that a new advance is God's will, then we say that it is a sign that God has spoken to that one, and is expecting him to obtain it by faith. We often remark that it is dangerous to keep pressing some new need in our meetings ; for the time is sure to come when we all turn round and say, ' All right, brother. Get it. If God has given you the vision, He has also given you the promises ! '

At this meeting Leslie Sutton was again urging the necessity of a new hostel. Half in fun, half seriously, I said, ' All right, then, Suto. If you are sure it is God's will, why not take it from Him ? Don't ask us to do it. Take it yourself.' Sutton answered, ' All right, I do.'

About three weeks after this conversation a man called on us. He owns property in the district and had come to ask some small point about a boundary line. It involved what are officially called ' The Stables,' No. 19, on a plot of land next door to our headquarters at No. 17 Highland Road. He did not know until then that we were renting it and had converted it into an office building. A week later he called again. To our amazement he made this remarkable statement, ' I have been studying all the property in this area, and I thought it might interest you to know that there are only two plots of land upon which the London County Council would allow the erection of a new building, and one is next door to you ; because those " Stables " are not reckoned as a house.' We had not mentioned to him our thought of building. The Crusade had occupied these houses some twenty years, during which no such information had been given us. Yet now, within a month of our entering into this transaction of faith with the Lord for a new building, we were gratuitously informed that the plot which we already rented was one of the only two in the district available for this purpose ! If some of us had doubts before, we could now plainly see that God was in this thing.

We now began to watch for the next moving of

the Spirit. Obviously money must come from somewhere, and it would need to be designated for a building at home : not a usual type of gift, for donors naturally prefer their money to go to the fields. Only a few weeks later it came as simply and naturally as the information about the ground. We received the news of the home-call of an old friend of the work, not a wealthy man. He had a small house at the other end of London. The remarkable thing was that, not only did he leave this to the Crusade *for use at the home end*, but with it a sum of about £1,200 for its upkeep. By the terms of the will we were informed that we could sell the house so long as we used the proceeds for the same object. The sale was effected, raising the total to nearly £2,000, specifically for a house at the home base. The actual money was not available at the moment, but, with the knowledge of its coming, we were able to use an equivalent sum during the interval. The unlikely had happened, just as if it had been a normal experience to receive such gifts.

The next step was obvious. With the good hand of our God thus on us, we were justified in going into details of the type of building we needed, and the cost. A three-storied house, to sleep 30, feed 60, and with a room to hold 100 for meetings would best suit us, but we discovered that the cost would be £4,000, double the sum we had received. As usual, we faced out this new problem at our morning meeting. It was not long before the Lord gave unexpected guidance. Among the candidates we often have men with practical experience of all kinds of trades, and someone proposed that we should deliberately ask the Lord to send candidates who could form a building team. As all work at headquarters is done on a voluntary basis unto the Lord alone, this would mean that there would be no wages to pay, and as wages are half the cost the £4,000 building could then be erected for the £2,000 we already had in hand. We all felt this to be the Lord's leading, and thenceforth brought this request daily to Him.

Meanwhile we delved further into practical details. There were the plans to be considered, then the purchase of material and the hire of equipment, such as scaffolding and a concrete mixer. If we amateurs had fully realized all that is involved in the erection of a modern building, which has to pass the tests of the County Council, we doubt that we ever would have launched out on it. Still the Lord saw the spark of living faith, and graciously and literally supplied above what we had asked or thought—an earnest Christian contractor who in one sweep took the oversight and handled all those problems which would have baffled us.

His call was remarkable. One of our number pointed out that we might have a difficulty in obtaining scaffolding, for usually a contractor will only employ his scaffolding on his own contracts. However, he said he knew a Christian contractor, Mr. Will Hopkins, who might hire or lend some out of sympathy with our objective. Mr. Hopkins came over to see us. Nothing was settled, but on his return home he fell sick and was a week in bed. There God spoke to him. Unknown to us, his business was in a bad way, for the building trade was suffering from serious depression. He was only employing some fifteen workmen instead of the usual eighty. 'At that time,' Mr. Hopkins told me later, 'we had secured a large contract. Then God said, "The hostel or the contract." For a week I completely lost the use of my legs. And God said, "See how dependent you are on Me. Will you give your skill and time for Me?" Of course I obliged.' We know no man who is more utterly obedient to God's voice when he is sure of His commands; and the consequence was an offer from 'Uncle Hoppy,' as we called him, not merely to loan the scaffolding, but to undertake the oversight of the whole building himself, to produce the plans, to obtain the right materials at cost price, and to loan any other necessities including a concrete mixer.

An unexpected delay followed. Twice over the London County Council rejected the plans. A year passed before they accepted the third set of drawings. Yet that delay was as much an answer to prayer as any of the previous deliverances. For by the end of the year, when we were all ready to build, without an effort or appeal to get any one, we had with us twelve men candidates for the fields. Of these actually six were experts in various phases of building, three bricklayers and three carpenters. One of

158

these, Wilfrid Watt, a nephew of Mr. Hopkins, had also received training which fitted him as a foreman. The building team was a reality.

The work began in January, 1937, and was finished by June, 1938. During that time, as the need arose and at the right moment, the Lord supplied no less than five more specialists. The first of these was in February, when 200 steel girders had arrived and were lying on the ground. It looked impossible that such dangerous and expert work could be carried through with a team of whom none had girder experience, when a Canadian joined us. We asked him what had been his work before going to Bible School, and he told us that among other things he had experience in erecting steel girders !

A few months later the electric lighting system had to be planned and installed. Just then two more young men joined us. They both turned out to be electrical engineers. Later on there was the central heating system, plumbing and sanitation to be done. For this big job the Lord had provided two plumbers, preparing for West Africa and India.

Finally, when the building had been completed, there was the interior decoration. An Australian mission, which has no English representative, asked us just at that time to test a candidate for them. On arrival I asked him his previous job and his answer was, of course, ' A house decorator ' !

It has been a special point in prayer that the Lord would enable this building team to do as thorough a job for Him as would be done by professional

159

builders. The acid test was the regular visits of the official inspector for the London County Council, who had power to order any alteration he liked. Naturally he was used to keeping a careful look-out for shoddy workmanship. As the weeks passed the Lord's good hand was seen here also, for the inspector became more of the friendly adviser than the critic. Later he said that he had not seen a more solid job done in all his experience.

In the process of building we used 200 girders, 70,000 bricks, 120 tons of concrete, 400 panes of glass. By the mercy of the Lord there were no accidents with the exception of a 10-foot fall by the foreman, resulting in a bruised back.

The crowning provision was a supply of furniture and a final anonymous gift of £300 to Leslie Sutton for the completion of the interior fittings. It was a most significant and wonderful seal of God's approval that this final gift should come direct to the one who had at the beginning taken the lead in launching out on His promises.

Of the twenty-six young men who at various times took part in the building, sixteen are to-day on the mission fields ; another has laid down his life in the Ivory Coast ; four are preparing to sail ; two are on the headquarters staff ; three have returned to witness for God in their own business. At the time of the opening of the new hostel, Mr. Hopkins, who had faithfully ' observed to do all that the Lord had commanded ' him, was employing 200 men where there had been fifteen. God had made the

The London Hostel, erected by a volunteer building-team of missionary candidates and headquarters staff, some of whom are seen in the lower picture

promise abundantly true, which he had attached to that condition, ' Then thou shalt make thy way prosperous and then thou shalt have good success.'

Not only is the hostel being used for the advance of the Gospel in unevangelized fields, but monthly conferences are being held, when friends gather as the Lord's guests in the Lord's house. With the concrete evidence of the Lord's faithfulness before them, they learn afresh what God will do through the least of His servants who will utterly trust and obey.

CHAPTER XVIII

WHERE WILL IT END?

ONE of the most inspiring experiences a Christian worker can have is to travel through the United States of America and see the number of young people in the Bible Institutes. It appears to a passing traveller as if every city of importance in that great country has its own School of the Scriptures, true to the Word of God, and in many cases with a numerous student body. If the traveller happens to be a missionary covetous of young life for the uttermost parts, a positive greed gets hold of him. Such were the feelings of Alfred Ruscoe when he went on a deputation tour to the United States and Canada in 1932.

Hearing, in addition, that many of these young people wanted to serve the Lord in the foreign field, but that the mission boards could not send them out to any great extent through lack of finance (for it was the time of the financial crisis in the States), the Lord gave him a definite vision of founding the Crusade in America and of seeing God do there what He was beginning to do in England, send out an army of Crusaders who had learned to trust the Lord alone for the supply of temporal needs.

A faith tour to Congo and South Africa intervening, it was not until 1936 that he was again brought face to face with God's word to him. At the time he was with a deputation team in England and dropped out ill. It was really inward conflict. He simply felt that he could not respond to such a big commission. God had taught him with us many new secrets of the life in the Spirit, where national as well as denominational barriers had dissolved into thin air ; but it was just the Moses experience common to all God-commissioned men. The call was clear, the anointing of the Spirit was his, the long disciplines which had brought him to an end of himself had been gone through ; there remained only that last wriggle of shrinking human nature, ' Who am I, that I should go ? ' But in three months he was ' through,' with the result that when he sailed it was not to make a success of the call, but with the success already his—by faith.

Actually a Canadian branch of the Crusade had been in existence for some years, and from 1931 Olive Ashton, a Canadian missionary on sick leave from the Congo, had opened a little home in Toronto where she trusted the Lord for the supply of personal needs, kept touch with a few friends all over the country, and sent forward some reinforcements. In 1934 she came over to spend a time in London headquarters, ultimately remaining on the staff, and leaving the management of our small affairs in the hands of a Christian friend, Mr. Harry Spence.

Then in August, 1936, Ruscoe crossed the Atlantic once again and arrived in Toronto. Those faithful workers had kept the flag flying in the day of small things, but now the Lord's time had come for something far larger—a work more in keeping with the promises of God and commensurate with the need of the unevangelized millions. Ruscoe knew it. It was just at that point that the conflict had raged. The Holy Spirit would not allow him to talk of his own weakness or plan for small results when He had said, 'Greater things shall ye do.' Nor would He allow him a single earthly prop, for by our self-governing principles Ruscoe had full responsibility for getting both guidance and supplies for the new work from God.

Welcomed into Mr. Spence's home, he thought he would begin in the usual way by looking for meetings and openings. The Holy Spirit checked him. Had he not come out to prove that the way to do God's work is to listen to His voice and only do the things He says ? Speaking to him one night through the story of the man who built his house on a rock, he was instructed to build up the new regime on a solid foundation of obedience and faith. The first step he was led to take was when, passing a good-sized house on College Street, he noticed a sign ' Room to Let ' and went in to see it. It was a large airy room on the second floor, and here the Spirit spoke and assured him that this was the place to begin in, even though there were no further rooms to let in the house. Securing some green boarding and tools, he screened off a small portion of the room to accommodate his camp bed, and another part was partitioned to install a second-hand cooking stove for light housekeeping. The remainder of the room was used to accommodate an office desk and chair. Into this he moved, and became man of all work— housemaid, janitor, cook, stenographer and secretary !

From this small beginning the work began to grow and the claims on his time increase. But, being far from strong, it soon became too much for him. From the beginning he had been most grateful for one source of steady help, in assistance with the bookkeeping from Mr. W. L. Kingdon (uncle of our first Canadian Crusader), and Daisy Kingdon of the Congo, who became the treasurer. There were also offers of stenographic help, but these were on the basis of an ordinary salary, and the Lord had made it plain that there was to be no paid staff. Just here came the first real test of faith. The devil mocked and said, 'You will never get any one to work for nothing over here, as they do in England.' But Ruscoe determined not to give in.

All that has happened since in the provision of the headquarters' staffs hung in the balance those days. Thank God he went through ; the battle was won and the answer began to appear. The first was a candidate for the field. When interviewed she turned out to be a stenographer and to have been called when in Bible School to live a life of faith. She saw this now temporarily to be God's work for her and came in daily. About the same time a young man who was a bookkeeper offered also to give daily help. Then another candidate arrived. Having no home in Toronto he had to be accommodated in the one room. He turned out to be quite a cook, and so was asked to disappear behind the screen and prepare the meals !

Ruscoe was now able to fulfil the desire of his heart and start W.E.C. morning prayers, ' spending unlimited time in facing out all problems in the presence of God. Last Friday they lasted until 12.15. There is absolutely nothing like this team work.'

By now they were becoming desperately in need of more room and were praying for an extension. ' There has been a wonderful conglomeration of jobs going on in the one room, and we must have more space.' The top flat, by the amount of tramping up the stairs which went on, ' seemed to be the headquarters for a certain national group in the city.' So they began to ask the Lord to find this group better quarters ! Ruscoe clinched it by writing home to his mother, saying that they would soon be in the top flat. Just after, however, a new cooking stove was seen to arrive and be carried upstairs, and the devil said, ' That's finished any idea of their moving ! ' Ruscoe's answer was, ' Lord, please find those other quarters both for them and their cooking stove ! ' On the first of the next month these folk gave in their notice to leave. Ruscoe heard the news from the landlady, who ' rang me up and told me this in a surprised tone, because she said they were staying on indefinitely. She said, " I think you must have prayed them out," to which I replied that I thought so too ! ' She then surprised him further by offering the whole house of three floors and thirteen rooms, which he accepted, leaving the ground floor with tenants until he needed it.

The heavens now opened on them. ' Three people are scrubbing away upstairs, cleaning the whole flat out, and one of them singing at the top of his voice. The place does really begin to feel more like ours. We have put in three beds, three dressers and several chairs. We have also had a splendid dinner service given us.' ' Many applications have come from one Bible School alone. I don't know what sort of a life I am going to have when they all congregate down here ! ' ' Coming into this H.Q. with a few dollars, the challenge soon came to start feeding a household by faith, and when this was accepted personal supplies came immediately from as far away as South Africa, and have been coming in ever since.'

' Last Monday I got a wonderful surprise package. If you don't know what a shower is, ask any of the Canadians. Some friends, with whom I have had much fellowship since my arrival here, invited me to a praise meeting down at the house. When I arrived I saw quite a crowd of people, but did not smell a rat ! I walked inside and sat down on the only available chair, and then at a given signal the folks started piling presents on top of me. You could have knocked me down with a feather. My, what a pile of stuff we had ! '

The story of Horace and Carol Davey has already been told in the chapter on Liberia. It was at this juncture that they came into the Canadian picture. It was through meeting Ruscoe, and catching a new vision of what God does through faith, that the two of them, with Percy Clubine, and joined by Ruscoe's first two candidates, Gertrude Woods and Cyril Holloway, formed the pioneer party for Liberia. At the same time there came a home reinforcement which brought a great accession of strength to Ruscoe's hands. The Rev. Edward Hancox, a Baptist minister, and his wife, had also been out with the Daveys in Liberia. Their hearts also had remained with Liberia, and when the Daveys heard the call to return, the Hancoxs were likewise called to stand behind them at the home end.

As the Daveys were joining up with the Crusade it meant the Hancoxs doing the same. There could be no half measures. If for the Daveys it meant a header into Liberia, for them it must mean a header into the home end of the Crusade. They had a comfortable little home of their own and had just been called to a church. There was also Mrs. Hancox's mother, Mrs. Paton, and a little baby. Everything was given up, the church and the home, and the whole family came bag and baggage into ' 163.' To the women especially it seemed like a nightmare to join such a household, pool their furniture, live day by day on what the Lord sent, with no allowance, but dependence on God direct for personal needs ; yet when I met them a year later, although the spiritual battles had been many, I do not know how many

times over they said that every department of their
life had been revolutionized and that they had never
known such joy before in their ministry. It was not
long before Mr. Hancox took charge of the deputation department, and Mrs. Hancox became house
mother.

Even this was only the beginning of blessings.
With the sailing of the first Liberian party, Ruscoe
was again left without a stenographer. Within
ten days a young lady from Winnipeg came to
Toronto, seeking employment in the office of a
Railway Department. She paid a visit to the W.E.C.
home to meet a candidate she knew, and at once
the Lord spoke and told her that this was His place
for her. The result was that a few days later Ann
Thomson became the first member of the permanent
office staff. Two more then joined, Edith John-
stone, a candidate for the field unable to go because
of ill-health, who helps Mrs. Hancox in the house ;
and Ethel Rodway, unable owing to ill-health to go
to Liberia, who is both a stenographer and in charge
of the Young Warriors' work. Finally, in 1938, a
clergyman of the Church of England, the Rev. Edwin
Gillman, and his wife and family, joined the headquarters' staff. Ruscoe must have been ' like them
that dream ' when he looked back over that first
two and a half years and realized that the Lord
had given him a thirteen-roomed house (for the
occupants of the ground floor left soon after) ; a
voluntary headquarters' staff of seven ; the opening
of a Canadian field ; and the sailing of eleven to the

various lands. The 'greater things' were coming rapidly into view.

He never wavered, however, in his conviction that his call was to open up work in the States. I had dropped hints that he had better remain in Canada, where he would pass muster, being a Britisher. But he would not. He was willing to start in Canada, but the United States was his main objective.

In this fresh advance, of such great importance, I was able to give him a helping hand. For years I also had seen the opportunities the States with her great population presented for world-wide evangelization. I often told Mrs. Grubb that I knew I should go to U.S.A., but the point was that I should know the Lord's time. To go in my own enthusiasm would mean hard work and doors difficult to open. If God sent me, the openings and opportunities would be there in His own abundant fashion.

What an open door it was when it came! In 1936 I received a request from Dr. and Mrs. Henry M. Woods, of Atlantic City, U.S.A., founders of the World-Wide Revival Prayer Movement, asking permission to publish the life of C. T. Studd as a gift edition to students, similar to the one published on the life of Hudson Taylor, which had been greatly used in calling out volunteers for China. Permission was given gladly and an edition of 10,000 copies soon exhausted, followed by another of 5,000. The challenge of C. T.'s life of sacrifice was tremendous throughout the country and continual testimonies are received of lives blessed and revolutionized.

Even then I had no inkling that God had anything further in this, until in 1937 I met Mrs. Woods in London. God then revealed it to both of us that the book should be followed by a visit to U.S.A. During that ten months, mainly through Mrs. Woods' kindness, I was able to address 600 meetings, and could have taken many more had there been time. Open doors indeed !

But all through the itinerary I always kept clearly before the Lord that my real objective was not to take meetings, but to find His choice for our first Crusade centre. Friendly and ' common sense ' suggestions were made, but it was the Lord's choice we wanted, and we kept telling Him and others that we could not decide till ' the cloud rested.' The guidance came as unexpectedly, yet unmistakably, as ever. When in North Carolina I was only passing through the city of Charlotte, speaking at the chapel service of a women's college. A woman 'phoned and asked me to call round before leaving the city, saying she wanted to know if a work of our kind could not be started in the city, because many Christian people there wanted to support an out-and-out faith missionary society. She offered to arrange a lunch meeting. At this the chairman of the Christian Business Men's Groups throughout the State came and said that, if we were to start in Charlotte, he would do his best to interest the Christian business men in the work. The fact that responsible Christian leaders desired us to settle among them was exactly the guidance we were seeking. It was just like the

Lord, for the Southern States was not the customary place for a new mission to open its headquarters in, and we could never have chosen it in our own wisdom.

In November, 1938, a ten-roomed house was secured in E. Fourth Street, standing in about two acres of ground. 'It was a queer feeling,' wrote Ruscoe, 'when a U.S. candidate and I occupied the empty house, expecting the Lord to fill it with furniture, staff and candidates. The day we went in, a dining-room table and an old couch were given to us. The latter, with a camp cot, were our only sleeping arrangements. We had no chairs to sit on, so we perched at the table on our suitcases. Then a family who were moving house found that some of their furniture was unsuitable for their new home and sent along a large office desk, dresser and double bed. Later some rockers were given which replaced the suitcases at meal times. One day a line of cars drew up outside and in came a number of women carrying parcels containing kitchen utensils, table-cloths, bed linen, etc. It was a " shower " given by a local women's Bible Class.' Within a few months the house was reasonably furnished, and in the same way the Lord has supplied the daily needs. Indeed the daily evidence of the faithfulness of God has been a blessing in the city and surrounding districts, and encouraged others to prove Him for themselves.

Yet this was only a step in the vision, the fullness of which the Lord had revealed to Ruscoe and me in two separate sections. While journeying in the north He laid it on me one day that if we would believe He would give 200 Crusaders from North America. I told Ruscoe, and he then told me what God had said to him, that he was to open four headquarters in the east, west, central and south of this vast country, and that He would supply the voluntary home staff necessary, numbering probably twenty. Of these Toronto and Charlotte are two, and the third has now been opened in Seattle, Washington. In addition to the voluntary staff of seven Canadians already mentioned, six Americans have either already joined the American staffs, or given up their positions in preparation for doing so, making a total of thirteen. Of these, two are a Lutheran minister and his wife, two a business man and his wife, and two other young women. What hath God wrought !

In the Antipodes, Mr. H. P. Smith and a Melbourne Council, reinforced now by a New South Wales Council, have sent forward ten workers with several more preparing to come. In New Zealand, more recently, the Rev. A. S. Wilson with a council have set to work vigorously and sent out already six Crusaders. In both these countries Crusade headquarters are soon to be opened along the same lines as in Britain and North America.

CHAPTER XIX

THE SECRET

I KNOW no more illuminating truth for our generation than the heights and depths of the 'mystery' which Paul said he was commissioned to reveal to the Gentiles—'Christ in you.' An unveiling of the fact that I am inwardly 'one'd' with Christ through the blood of His atonement, a realization that it is a fact, not a distant ideal, a bursting through of the suggestions of world and flesh and Devil that there is still a gulf or distance between us; this opens wide the gates for the flood tides of conscious enablement. All power is mine if He is my life; all guidance is mine if His mind indwells mine; all authority is mine if I share His throne as a king and command deliverances according to His instructions to me (Mark xi. 22-24).

I ought to fulfil the task given me. God expects me to. I have no excuses for failure. God has not given me the spirit of fear, but of love, power and sanity. We are set in our day and generation to be overcomers, not to sail through calm seas, but to walk on storms, to replace need with supply, to transform aspiration into realization. The language of defeatism, fear, lack, weakness is not to be in our vocabulary. 'Let us go up at once and possess it, for we are well able to overcome it. As for these giants, they are bread for us,' we say with sturdy

174

Caleb. We are to act as the men of faith of old ; we are to visualize our goal in clear outline ; we are to take it for granted that we shall reach it, for have we not both the commission and anointing of God ? We are to lay our plans, build our organizations, produce our written and verbal pronouncements, pray our prayers, do our work, not as those who will fail and fall by the way, but as those who will finish the work we have been sent to do, as did our Lord and Saviour.

Our own goal is clear. We have made it plain in these pages, and in the attaining of it we have endeavoured to put these great truths into practice, and have found God's seal on them beyond our powers of description or words of adequate praise. Inwardly there has been the calm of a life at rest : in the family life of our far-flung brotherhood there has been a new grasp and understanding of the principles of open, happy fellowship, freeing us from internal strife to engage the true enemy of souls : outwardly in the battle there has been the conscious enduement which turns the contradiction of sinners, the oppositions of Satan, the stresses of pioneer life or financial need, into the fuel for triumphant faith.

Mistakes there have been. Many things might have been done better. It is of the Lord's mercy that He uses such as us, and we would always be open to the checks and warnings of the Spirit whether directly or by other members of the Body. Still, as Jack Harrison wrote after C. T. Studd's

death, words with which we closed his life story,
' God enabling us, we shall go on ! '

The goal is clear before us—the adequate occupation of all those areas in which we already have a
footing, the building of churches of Christ in them
until the natives themselves can assume full responsibility, and the entry into any other such unevangelized areas not being worked by other missions. By
God's grace we keep that and nothing less ever before
us as not only our responsibility but as the task for
which we are ' well able ' in Christ.

My prayer is that through these pages some of you,
my readers, as a personal responsibility may also be
commissioned to take this preaching of the Gospel
to all who have never yet heard it.   To others of you
God may speak in another way : He may open your
eyes to your resources in Christ and may be telling
you to see to it that the same kind of works of the
Spirit take place in your sphere.   To you also comes,
as to us, the word of the prophet of old, ' The people
that do know their God shall be strong and do
exploits.'

One fundamental fact remains to be stated.
There is a background to the manifestation of the
mighty works of God through a human channel.
Underlying resurrection is death. Paul to possess
all things had nothing ; to make many rich was
poor ; to be powerful and wise had become foolish
and weak ; to be re-made had been broken. To
share the intimate fellowship of a Saviour he went
the way of saviourhood, ' suffered the loss of all

things,' ' became conformable to death.' We know and can employ through the Spirit the powers of the world to come in the measure that we have died out to enslavement to the possessions, glories, ways of this world. It is a real death, as prelude to a real new life. The Lord Christ made some strange statements, such as that it costs some an eye or limb to enter the Kingdom, that a disciple must forsake all, must ' hate ' loved ones, possessions, life. By this He meant that such an one must pass through fires in which the selfish claims of natural loves and the selfish hold on the ' good things ' of life, not to speak of the bad, must be burnt out to make room for the influx of supernatural grace, vision and resources. Holy and hidden mystery—that through the Cross is power, through the Cross glory, through the Cross joy, through the Cross fruitfulness.

God grant that we may be of this company of the abundant life, with a gaiety that is irrepressible, an attraction that is irresistible (through ourselves to Him), an adventurousness, an optimism and a courage that strike the deep chords of human nature ; yet withal with a purity, intensity, meekness and altruism which are not of this world, but are a sweet savour of Christ, both of life unto life and death unto death. These are they who in every generation ' turn the world upside down ' and make preparation for the glorious day of Christ's personal appearing. Even so come, Lord Jesus.

THE FORM OF GOVERNMENT USED IN THE WORLDWIDE EVANGELIZATION CRUSADE

FOR the sake of those interested in the more technical side of missions, the following description of the methods of government in the Crusade may be helpful.

It is rare to find a mission of the interdenominational type, such as our own, which has not known internal strife. Most of it is due to failure in striking the balance between individual liberty and submission to authority. The great denominations, in the main, have well-developed systems of authority, strengthened by long tradition to which their members are accustomed to bow, and which has its own abuses as well as uses.

The interdenominational movement is a newer growth. Many of those who join are of the free-lance type, whose emphasis on personal allegiance to Christ the Head of the Body is not always healthily counterbalanced by the equally essential truth of loyalty to the fellow members of the Body. Equally, the form of government is often immature, varying from dictatorship to democratic control. The clash of the two, undisciplined membership with immature government, has often set light to revolt.

We have had our full share of it, of both kinds, failures in wise direction and individuals impatient of control. This has driven us through the years to institute a thorough method of testing candidates and to make a very careful examination of the best form of government for the Crusade. In the days of our founder, authority lay in an imperfectly defined balance between the president on the field and the executive committee in London. At his death it was felt by all our members that a founder was a privileged person, and that no one could exactly take his place ; so the position of president was never filled.

At the same time it was unanimously felt that to vest final authority in an executive committee which consisted of friends of the Crusade, but not whole-time workers in it, was not the most suitable form of government. All due regard was paid to the friends, men and women of God, who had faithfully served the Crusade as executive members, nor was there any feeling but of deepest gratitude to each of them ; but the principle was to our minds fundamentally wrong. We could not see, and we felt that experience had proved it, that outside brethren in Christ, sane and experienced though they may be, could really feel the pulse and find the mind of the Spirit moving in the hearts of those to whom He had given a life and death commission in the Crusade. It seemed to us that the whole principle of Scripture is that God reveals His mind concerning a piece of work specifically to those whom He has commissioned to do it, and that all the great Christian organizations had proved this to be true by giving authority to and taking guidance from leaders in their own ranks.

We did not quickly act on these convictions. The first stage we have already mentioned in the non-appointment of a new president. The second was about a year later, when the workers on the Congo, then called the Heart of Africa Mission, communicated to us in London their decision to be self-governing so far as all field affairs were concerned, recognizing the home base to be equally self-governing in home affairs. Mutual faith in each other was the necessary foundation for the new relationship, for while we at home must trust them to direct the field affairs wisely and well, they must trust us in the very important points of the distribution of finances and selection of candidates. Dictatorship on the field was avoided by placing in the missionaries' hands the right to replace a leader, if thought necessary, and to reinforce him with a field committee.

Taking the cue from the Congo, three years later we adopted their constitution for all new fields and home bases. We became a completely self-governing Crusade. Each new field, so soon as it is properly established, say after two years, has full control over its own affairs. Each home base likewise. All are bound together by loyalty to our Principles and Practices, which is a simple outline of faith and conduct with as few rules as possible.

We have now had the opportunity of trying out this form of constitution for seven years since the Congo adopted it. We have extended during this period from one field to 11 and from 38 Crusaders to 200, and we can only say that there is a healthy feeling of unity, loyalty and liberty between us all. Relationships are as perfect as could be between fields and home bases. We believe that the whole Crusade feel that this way of government is the mind of God for us. So far from drying up the interchange of opinion and advice between fields and home, we find that we all are far more open to talk things over and accept suggestions, when, instead of having a decision thrust on us, we are each at liberty to find the mind of God respectively in our own spheres.

We find also that by this form of self-government here is much more incentive both to sacrifice and advance. When the reins are in the hands of a council drawn from outside the ranks of the full-time workers, we find that the brethren on the council very naturally are reluctant to ask the workers to risk financial insecurity by the sending of reinforcements or the opening of new fields, when they themselves cannot take the same share in the sacrifice. But when decisions lie with those who pay the price of them, it is easy to make them, for naturally all are equally ready to embrace the way of the Cross, and are not asking of others beyond what they are doing themselves.

For final security in the Crusade, authority has been vested in a Leaders' Council, consisting of the leaders of all fields and home bases. It would entail great expense for these to meet; they have never done so yet, and we hope will never need to—for only a severe crisis would make it essential.

We find the effect of this constitution to be as that of the United States of America or the British Commonwealth of Nations. Just as each member of the Commonwealth is bound to the other by voluntary ties of affection and convenience, and not by compulsion, so are we ; and just as the result in the Empire is a sense of unity and liberty, so also do we find it. If this form of government has a weakness, it is the fact that a mission consists not only of the full-time workers, but also of subscribers and praying friends, and that the latter may feel more confidence if they have some form of representation by a committee drawn from their ranks. Perhaps so. Perhaps the ideal is an executive committee of the workers themselves in each sphere and an advisory general committee from the ranks of home supporters. We ourselves are tending in that direction by holding conferences of our provincial representatives, where they can be free to express their views on the conduct of the work. We are open to advice and alteration in order to obtain the best possible constitution for the furtherance of the work. However, we remain as firmly convinced as ever that authority in each sphere should rest with those who do the work.

In home countries where we have as yet no full-time representative or headquarters staff, responsibility has been carried by friends of the Crusade, who have done magnificent work by forming councils and forwarding a steady stream of new workers to the fields, such as Mr. H. P. Smith and the Australian Council, the Rev.

A. S. Wilson and the New Zealand Council. In both these cases they are looking to the day when, in co-operation with them, W.E.C. headquarters with full-time workers have been established in their respective countries.

The question might arise in some minds that, while a field is a community of workers and therefore it is easy to understand authority in the hands of a field leader and committee, at home the case is different, for there is no body of workers. In whose hands, then, does home leadership lie ? We have found the solution to this in our honorary headquarters' staff, the upbuilding of which is described in Chapter VI.

APPENDIX II

WHAT IS A FAITH MISSION?

I WAS speaking at a city church in U.S.A. The minister knew next to nothing about the Crusade and asked me rather frigidly, ' Do you represent one of those faith missions? ' ' Yes, the W.E.C. is a so-called faith mission,' I replied. He was obviously pleased. ' I am glad to hear you say that, because all missions are faith missions, and I don't think it right that the so-called faith missions should monopolize this name as if no others had faith.'

There is a sense in which he was obviously right. No missionary society would have come into being or continued true to its calling if it had not been founded on faith.

Yet there is also a specialized sense in which interdenominational missions have emphasised faith to the point that they have been dubbed ' Faith Missions.' The explanation is to be found in the reason for their existence. The great denominational missions form the foundation and largely the superstructure of the modern missionary movement. Their resources have been drawn from their home churches, and their extensions on the fields have been dependent on their income at home. Their financial structure has been on the simple basis of a fixed rate of salary, an annual estimate of expenditure, and activities generally up to the limit•of their budget. When they found they had reached that limit they ceased to advance.

When the interdenominational missions entered the arena their objective was to occupy regions to which the other missions had not been able to penetrate. But they had no home constituency behind them for financial

183

support. Therefore they could not have come into existence had not men arisen, such as George Müller and Hudson Taylor, who expounded a new solution to the financial problem, that of activity based on faith in the promises of God for all supplies, and who gave practical proof of its workability in their own sphere of action.

Their disciples have been the multitude of organizations which constitute the faith missions of to-day and which have made an outstanding contribution towards the completion of world-wide evangelization.

It is obvious that the manner of supply from God to man is composed of a trinity—a Source, a channel and a recipient. The faith principle, while recognizing the visible channel, concentrates itself on the invisible Source, the Heavenly Father.

Great care has to be taken to maintain our hearts and minds free from financial aims in our activities. Our meetings and literature are used to get our audiences rightly adjusted to God, to bring spiritual vision and sense of responsibility to them, leaving it to the Holy Spirit to move individuals to pray, work, give or go. We avoid financial appeals and collections, even sometimes to the inconvenience of the audiences, in order to keep ourselves financially with a single eye on God. Yet we realize that in all probability He will use the meetings and literature to supply our needs ; but it will be in His own way and time.

It may be asked, Why do we use all this scrupulousness over appeal for funds ? Why do we make so much of this principle of faith in finance ? For this vital reason. If the mission programme is based on God's invisible resources, then new projects and advances will be continually undertaken on the basis of an inexhaustible supply. If the human channel is the basis of calculation, then advance will be up to the limit of the human supply. Herein lies the acid test of a genuine 'faith' work. There is a sense in which my friend the Presbyterian minister is right—all missions have faith. There is also a sense in which the genuine 'faith mission' does exercise a peculiar quality of faith, a re-discovery from the Scriptures which has enabled a section of Christ's church, not to rival and certainly not to trespass on the work of the great denominational missions, but to supplement and, we believe, soon help them to complete the church's great commission.

We ourselves have endeavoured to adhere completely to these foundation principles of faith by advancing to an unlimited extent, without regard to the size of our budget. Each new field has been started on nothing beyond the first hundred or two pounds for the outgoing of the first workers. Not only that, but the possibility of a new field drawing funds away from an old has not been allowed to weigh with us. The practical method by which this policy has been carried through is by having no fixed standards of allowance. Had we those, we should be continually faced with the necessity of financing our existing commitments before taking on others. But we have agreed that if our sole concern is the spread of the Gospel, we have no right to lay down a fixed standard of living.

Admittedly it has often meant stringency and sacrifice. Crusaders accept that as their privilege, as part of the necessary losing of their lives that the world may find life. The Crusade adopts voluntarily for Christ's sake both at home and abroad the simplest standards of living compatible with health and efficiency. By God's grace and strength we are even prepared, if need be, to go farther and share with the Apostle Paul in 'hunger, thirst and nakedness,' to bring our Redeemer the reward of His sufferings and to save precious souls.

Fields at present occupied by

THE WORLDWIDE EVANGELIZATION CRUSADE

Which also incorporates the Christian Literature Crusade and
The Leper Crusade

AFRICA	Crusaders	SOUTH AMERICA	Crusaders
Belgian Congo	60	Republic of Colombia	38
Ivory Coast	20	INDIA	
Spanish Guinea	7	United Provinces	15
Senegal	3	Nepal Border	4
Portuguese Guinea	2	Tibetan Border	2
Liberia	23	Kashmir	15
Gold Coast	5	WEST INDIES, Dominica	5

FIELDS IN PROCESS OF OCCUPATION

Chinese-Tibetan Border — Canary Islands — Martinique

HOME BASES

United States of America — Canada — Great Britain
Australia — New Zealand

Voluntary Home Workers   78   Recruits for various fields   28
Total — 305

FOUNDER C. T. STUDD

OBJECT

The Evangelization of every part of the Unevangelized World
in the shortest possible time.

DOCTRINAL BASIS

Commonly called the Five Smooth Stones

1. Absolute faith in the Deity of each Person of the Trinity.
2. Absolute belief in the full inspiration of the Old and New Testament Scriptures.
3. Vow to know and to preach none other save Jesus Christ and Him crucified.
4. Obedience to Christ's command to love all who love the Lord Jesus sincerely without respect of persons, and to love all men.
5. Absolute faith in the will, power, and providence of God to meet our every need in His service.

North American Addresses

UNITED STATES

8864 Germantown Avenue   1322 East Fourth Street
Philadelphia 18, Pa.   Charlotte 4, N. C.
937—12th Ave., N., Seattle 2, Wash.

CANADA

11 Roxborough Street, E.   Suite 1, Thomson Block
Toronto 5, Ontario   Calgary, Alberta

General Secretary...................ALFRED W. RUSCOE
Secretary.................................EDWIN GILLMAN

LaVergne, TN USA
07 December 2010

207735LV00009B/108/A

9 781436 709194